The Practice Educator's Handbook
Second Edition

SARAH WILLIAMS
AND
LYNNE RUTTER

Series Editors: Keith Brown and Steven Keen

Los Angeles | London | New Delhi
Singapore | Washington DC

Learning Matters
An imprint of SAGE Publications Ltd
1 Oliver's Yard
55 City Road
London EC1Y 1SP

SAGE Publications Inc.
2455 Teller Road
Thousand Oaks, California 91320

SAGE Publications India Pvt Ltd
B 1/I 1 Mohan Cooperative Industrial Area
Mathura Road
New Delhi 110 044

SAGE Publications Asia-Pacific Pte Ltd
3 Church Street #10-04 Samsung Hub
Singapore 049483

Editor: Luke Block
Development editor: Lauren Simpson
Production controller: Chris Marke
Project management: Deer Park
Productions, Tavistock, Devon
Marketing manager: Tamara Navaratnam
Cover design: Wendy Scott
Typeset by: PDQ Typesetting Ltd,
Newcastle-under-Lyme
Printed by: MPG Printgroup, UK

Library of Congress Control Number:
2013930250

British Library Cataloguing in Publication
Data
A catalogue record for this book is available
from the British Library

ISBN 978 1 44626 660 1
ISBN 978 1 44626 668 1 (pbk)

Contents

Foreword from the Series Editors

Practice education is at the forefront of developing social work practice and the first edition of this book was written to support the delivery and development of the Practice Education Framework. This subsequently led to the development of the Practice Educator Professional Standards (PEPS).

PEPS are now being implemented and this edition has been written with a view to supporting anyone with a role in practice education including people working towards becoming practice educators and meeting the PEPS, experienced practice educators who would like to update and further develop their practice and social workers supporting and assessing newly qualified social workers (NQSW) during their Assessed and Supported Year in Employment (ASYE), as well as people with a strategic interest in practice education.

The book has been fully updated to provide guidance and support to practice educators working within the new Professional Capabilities Framework (PCF) to assess social workers at all stages of their career but with a specific focus on students and NQSWs. A new chapter has been included on assessment that looks at the implications of the PCF for the assessment of professional practice and introduces and explores the concept of holistic assessment.

This edition is full of practical tasks, ideas, guidance and implications for practice educators. We trust that this helps to encourage the social work profession to reach even higher standards.

All texts in this series have been written by people with a passion for excellence in social work. This book is no different. Other books in this series may also be of value to you as a practice educator, as they are written to inform, inspire and develop social work practice.

Professor Keith Brown and Dr Steven Keen
National Centre for Post Qualifying Social Work, Bournemouth University

Introduction

Structure of the book

In the opening chapter we set the scene by providing an opportunity to find out more about how professional development can be supported through learning that takes place in work-based settings. A more theoretical approach is taken here, which helps develop an understanding of what work-based learning is, why such importance is placed on this type of learning in the development of professional competence and capability, and how practice learning can be effectively facilitated.

The book then follows the domains set out in the Practice Educator Professional Standards for Social Work (PEPS) (CSW, 2012) with four key parts.

- Part One. Domain A: Organise opportunities for the demonstration of assessed competence in practice.
- Part Two. Domain B: Enable learning and professional development in practice.
- Part Three. Domain C: Manage the assessment of learners in practice.
- Part Four. Domain D: Effective continuing performance as a practice educator.

As each domain covers large areas of practice, we have split each of these main parts into a number of manageable chapters. You can read a part from start to finish or you can dip into a chapter depending on your specific interest or the amount of time you have available.

The terms 'work-based learning' and 'practice learning' are both used to describe the learning that takes place within a work setting. Generally speaking, however, there are no agreed definitions for either of these terms and they are frequently used interchangeably (Nixon and Murr, 2006). Therefore, throughout this book we will refer to all learning that is located in the workplace as 'work-based learning'.

Who is this book aimed at?

This book has been written for busy social workers involved in supporting, enabling and assessing learners in the workplace. It is aimed primarily at people with responsibility for either qualifying social worker students or newly qualified social workers (NQSWs) during their first year of professional practice but it will also be of interest to those with responsibility for other professional learners such as students from other professions, people undertaking post-qualifying awards and those undertaking other forms of continuous professional development.

The book has been written specifically to support those undertaking practice educator awards which meet the staged requirements of the Practice Educator Professional Standards (CSW, 2012) and will be particularly useful for social workers who are new to a practice education role. It will also be of interest to more experienced practice educators seeking support to reflect critically on their practice and further develop their professional capability.

This second edition has been fully updated to provide guidance and support for both new and experienced practice educators working within the Professional Capabilities Framework (PCF)

(CSW, 2012). Particular emphasis is given to holistic assessment – with a new chapter to introduce and explore the concept at the start of Part Three.

How will the book support your practice?

We aim to present an easy-to-read book that will challenge you to take a critical, evidence-informed approach to your thinking and to your practice. Although the book will give you some useful ideas to use within your work with learners, it will not simply provide you with a 'bag of tricks' that can be pulled out and applied in an unthinking manner. It blends practical information and advice with material aimed at developing an understanding of key concepts and research that will encourage you to think about how and why adults learn in a professional context and how their practice can be assessed fairly and accurately. Throughout the book we have included examples drawn from our own practice and life experiences that aim to illustrate how we, as individuals, may have approached a particular situation. These examples represent just one view on practice and are intended to provide a starting point for you to critically think through your own approaches.

This book should therefore be seen as a handbook to guide your thinking rather than as a textbook concentrating on delivering content. It attempts to provide sufficient theory and discussion to help you gain new understanding in enabling the learning of others but does not give a comprehensive coverage of the literature in this complex area (that has been provided by a number of other excellent books). It uses activities and reflection points to encourage reflection on application to your own areas of practice as part of your development as a practice educator. Research summaries are also included throughout. A summary is provided at the end of Chapter 1 and for each of the following four parts of the book to provide a quick outline of the main ideas presented. Suggestions for further reading are also provided to enable you to explore issues raised in greater depth and extend your knowledge further.

This book will obviously support the development of practice education knowledge and skills but will also support some wider professional development. The integration of practice education within qualified social workers' professional roles can be seen as a natural extension in many respects. Skills and abilities required for the enabling of others through a learning and development process are obviously aligned with those used for social work with people who use social services (e.g. use of discretion, anti-discriminatory practice) and with those used when working alongside other professionals (e.g. communication, diplomacy). It is apparent that much prior experience will be relevant to this subject area and a great deal of material that is covered in this book and in associated programmes will be transferable to other areas of practice, such as supervision and management, as well as to direct work with service users and carers.

Chapter 1
Practice educators and work-based learning

Introduction

Have you ever spent time considering what makes you special? Not you as a person (although we are sure that you are), but you as a social worker. What knowledge, skills and attributes enable you to undertake the difficult job of supporting and safeguarding some of the most vulnerable people in society? How did you get to the point in your professional development that you have reached today? How did you gain your knowledge, build your skills and develop your attributes? How have other people supported you in your development?

In this opening chapter we will consider these fundamental questions and explore some of the theories that have been developed to explain how people like you make the journey from novice to expert within a professional role. We will argue that achieving 'competence' in specific areas of practice is a useful part of this process – but that competence alone is not enough to ensure that social workers are effective within their complex and challenging roles. We will consider what it means to be a professional, what knowledge, skills and attributes professionals need to function effectively and most importantly how that knowledge and those skills and attributes are acquired and developed. Towards the end of the chapter we will look at the role of the practice educator in facilitating learning and assessing practice and we will provide an opportunity for you to reflect on your own experiences and on the values that will provide a foundation for your work with learners.

This chapter provides a substantial amount of important, underpinning material which is explored and developed over six sections.

- What is work-based learning?
- The role of work-based learning in social work education.
- Becoming a professional – introducing the concept of professional capability.
- Developing professional capability through work-based learning.
- The Professional Capabilities Framework (CSW, 2012).
- The role of the practice educator in supporting work-based learning.

ACTIVITY 1.1

According to the report of the Social Work Task Force (2009, p5), social workers need confidence in their own skills, purpose and identity...

How do you think that work-based learning can begin to give people confidence in their own skills and an understanding of their purpose and identity in the interventions that they make with service users and their carers?

Comment

As someone with personal experience of social work (or other professional) education you will already have some ideas that will help you to answer the questions in this activity. However, you will probably know, or at the very least suspect, that they are very big questions and ones that have no clear-cut or simple answers.

What is work-based learning?

When first considering work-based learning, most people think about formal arrangements for professional or vocational development such as student placements or courses. Although these have an important role to play, there is another, much broader way of thinking about work-based learning that fits better with recent research on professional development (Eraut, et al., 1998; Wenger, 2000; Ford, et al., 2005; Nixon and Murr, 2006).

Although formal opportunities for learning, such as the qualifying social work degree and post-qualifying courses, have an important role in professional development, they are by no means the only ways that social workers and other professionals learn. And that is because in the workplace learning is happening pretty well all of the time. Whenever something new is encountered there is the potential to learn from it – even familiar situations offer opportunities for further developing knowledge and skills. Despite the fact that many of these learning opportunities are informal and unplanned, they can and do play a fundamental role in professional learning and development (Eraut, et al.,1998; Wenger, 2000).

It is worth remembering that even the most formal learning situations include significant informal learning elements – think about coffee breaks during seminars where you have the opportunity to talk about the material presented by the facilitator with your colleagues. The informal chat is an important part of the learning process because it helps you to think through new information, consider how that new information changes your existing ideas and form and test your own new 'theories'. Similarly, in a work-based setting informal learning can enhance and reinforce more formal learning experiences. For example, a student can learn a great deal from shadowing an experienced worker and reflecting on their observation after the event with either the worker or their practice educator as part of a formal learning opportunity. But the learning from that experience does not necessarily end there – later in the day or even later in the week the student may be chatting to someone about the things they have been doing and this casual conversation may lead to a new insight into the work that the student had observed. This may be because the person they are talking to helps them to understand a different perspective, or provides some new information, or may just ask questions in a way that encourages a deeper understanding. In work-based settings most learning occurs through a blend of formal and informal experiences, some of which may not even be recognised explicitly by learners as part of their learning process.

Implications for practice educators

There are two main implications of understanding the importance of informal learning in the workplace. Firstly, because informal learning is often an important part of the overall learning process, you need to pay attention not just to the formal ways that people learn but also to the informal. Secondly, because informal learning is an important way that we all learn at work, it is important for you to think about other ways that you can use your practice education skills – even in situations where you do not have a formal 'enabling' role. Although the main focus of this book is on working with social work students and newly qualified social workers, you as a skilled practice educator can also informally support the learning of colleagues and other professionals as part of your everyday professional practice.

Comment

Informal methods could include *ad hoc* conversations with colleagues in the office or in the car, learning through practice experience, learning from discussions with service users, observing or working alongside colleagues, attendance at meetings, visits to other agencies, etc. Informal learning has some strengths because it can expose people to a wide variety of approaches and ideas and can be a very efficient and relevant way to learn. However, you do need to be wary of informal learning that passes on poor practice through habit or the adoption of uncritical approaches and ideas, and you also need to be aware that informal learning can sometimes be incomplete or only partially understood.

When you are talking to people, the skills you have developed as a practice educator can help you to enable them to be more analytical and critical in their thinking. This may help them to learn more from their experiences. Encouraging learning to be shared with others can help teams to learn and develop more effectively. Eraut (1994) stresses the importance of informal learning as part of professional development, suggesting that something like 80 per cent of all learning happens in this way.

The role of work-based learning in social work education

Work-based learning is not a new concept, and learning within work-based environments has traditionally underpinned many professional and vocational learning programmes, including social work. However, the fundamental importance of learning that actually takes place in the workplace has recently been much more widely recognised (GSCC, 2006; Nixon and Murr, 2006; Social Work Task Force, 2009). The government's intentions were first made absolutely clear in the Department of Health requirements for the social work degree, which state that *practice is central to the new degree, with academic learning supporting practice rather than the other way round* (DoH, 2002, p1). The continuing commitment to work-based learning was also evident in the requirements for post-qualifying education, in which the General Social Care Council emphasised that it was an essential element of all continuing professional development (GSCC, 2005). Recent changes to continuing professional development (CPD) requirements for social workers have again placed learning from practice at centre stage, with the College of Social Work (CSW) setting up online communities of practice to enable social workers to share experiences and learn from each other (CSW, 2012).

It seems instinctively obvious that professional and vocational education should have a significant element of learning and assessment 'on the job'. If we buy a new car, we want to know that it has been thoroughly road-tested. Few of us would be happy to buy a car on the strength that 'on paper' the engineers thought that it would be reliable, efficient and would keep us safe. Road testing allows the engineers to fine-tune their product, to make improvements and to assess the overall performance of the car in the environment in which it will be used. Similarly, it makes sense for professionals who carry responsibility for the safety and security of vulnerable people to have an opportunity to 'fine-tune' their skills and test-drive their knowledge in a real-life setting. After all, reading about how to communicate with a service user is very different from actually being in a room with a distressed person with whom you need to engage. Work-based learning provides opportunities for learners to find out more about the realities of practice, extend their knowledge and skills, make improvements to their performance and be assessed actually doing the job that they are being prepared for.

The literature on professional education strongly supports the use of work-based learning (Grey, 2002). Listed below are just a few of the reasons why.

- Learning occurs through involvement in real-life situations and learners are gaining skills and knowledge which will help them carry out real-life tasks which will be applicable in their future professional role. Learning will be perceived as 'relevant' and this will increase the learner's motivation to learn and increase the chance that new learning will be remembered and consolidated (Knowles, 1990).

- Learning generally occurs through experience of working in complex and multi-contextual situations. This experience will tend to encourage learners to learn deeply, seeing links between new and existing knowledge and analysing the results of their actions in practice (Moon, 1999).

- Learning is often centred on work that the learner would be doing anyway, and it therefore carries the added advantage of being efficient in terms of time and effort, as learning and working can be carried out simultaneously.

However, there are some potential areas of difficulty with work-based learning that can impact negatively on the quality of the overall learning experience (Grey, 2002). Listed below are a few of the problems associated with work-based learning.

- The learning environment can be difficult to predict and control, leading to potential difficulties in ensuring that learning experiences are sufficient and appropriate for the learner's needs.

- Successful learning will be dependent on a number of factors including the motivation, confidence and competence of the learner; the provision of an appropriate degree of challenge; the micro-culture of the learning environment; and the way that the learner is managed and supported (Eraut, et al., 1998).

- Learning and the needs of learners will often take second place in social work and similar work-based learning situations where service user's and carers' needs are paramount. Short-term organisational needs are often prioritised over what are generally perceived as longer-term development needs. For instance, this can lead to the cancellation of supervision sessions or specific learning opportunities because of competing priorities on time, and little or no support or time for workers to reflect on their practice experiences.

ACTIVITY 1.3

Think back to your own experiences of work-based learning and choose an experience that you have had as a learner.

Read again the bullet points above that describe the advantages and disadvantages of work-based learning. Were any of the points raised particularly pertinent to your own learning experience?

How will thinking about this experience influence your future practice when you are supporting the learning of others?

Comment

Your own experiences of learning will influence your approach as a practice educator. Reflecting on these experiences will help you to understand where some of your views have come from and allow you to take a more critical stance towards those views. You may have had experiences of finding it difficult to complete a direct observation during a placement as a student because service users didn't turn up for appointments. This experience may have made you reflect on how you will support students to organise direct observations in your workplace.

Becoming a professional – introducing the concept of professional capability

The modern face of social work and the implications for social work learning

Before we can start to think about how social workers learn, we need to briefly explore some of the current challenges faced by the profession. This will help us to understand more about the role that social work students and newly qualified social workers are being prepared to fulfil. It will also help us to understand more why ongoing professional development for qualified workers is now more important than ever.

Social work has always been a challenging profession, but it could be argued that the pace of change in modern life and the complexities of our current society have led to a step change in the expectations being placed on social workers and other allied professionals (Doel, et al., 2002; Postle, et al., 2002; Brown, et al., 2005). Cherry (2005) believes that the complexity of working contexts and the speed of change faced by modern professionals 'defies prediction' and makes the task of social work much more difficult now than in the past. There are frequent changes to legislation and policies, together with demographic and structural changes within communities, which have led to the need for social workers to provide services for people with multiple and diverse needs.

The expectation that all professionals will be evidence-informed in their approach to practice has increased the pressures for practitioners to keep knowledge and skills current and to further develop areas of specialist knowledge (Gould, 2000; SCIE, 2004; SWRB, 2010). Social workers need to be able to work inter-professionally in a wide variety of complex settings and be equipped to problem-solve in unpredictable situations that can require the acquisition, evaluation and application of new knowledge almost on a daily basis (Nixon and Murr, 2006). To add further complications, social workers often practise in contexts where much of their work is driven by 'top-down' policy with targets set at a national level. Workloads and stress levels are high and social workers often feel that there is little scope for working creatively to meet service users' and carers' needs (Walker, et al., 2008).

Given the new challenges faced by the profession, it should not really be surprising that things go wrong and in recent years the social work profession has been placed under the spotlight on a number of occasions and been found seriously wanting (Laming, 2003, 2009). As a result of serious government and public concerns about the competence and effectiveness of the profession, the Social Work Task Force was asked to make recommendations that would lead to improvements in the quality of service provision (Social Work Task Force, 2009). Several of these recommendations are currently being implemented and are playing an important role in reshaping social work education. These include:

- a new set of professional standards for social workers at all stages of their careers – the Professional Capabilities Framework (CSW, 2012);
- a review of the qualifying degree with tighter specification of admissions and content;
- improvements to practice education;
- a new set of professional standards for practice educators – the Practice Educator Professional Standards (PEPS) (CSW, 2012);
- an assessed first year in practice for newly qualified social workers;
- a more coherent and effective continuing professional development framework for qualified workers.

The ultimate aims of these reforms are to make social work education and professional development 'fit for purpose' and to fully equip social workers at all stages of their careers with appropriate knowledge, skills and attributes to be effective in their role in this rapidly evolving and complex work climate.

But what are the knowledge, skills and attributes that social workers need today? How can they be developed? Can an understanding of these issues help make social work education 'fit for purpose'?

ACTIVITY **1.4**

Think back over your career and identify three skills that have been particularly valuable to you in dealing with complex situations.
How do you think you developed these skills? Can you identify any particular learning experiences that helped you develop them?

Comment

This activity has been designed to help you to reflect on how you work in complex situations and identify which particular skills you feel are most valuable to you. Although everyone will have different ideas, we would expect you to identify skills such as problem-solving, critical analysis, decision-making, communication and active listening.

The challenge of making social work education 'fit for purpose' – is competence enough?

Historically, one of the biggest problems with attempts to make social work education 'fit for purpose' has been the continuing disagreement about what exactly that purpose is (Thompson, 2005; Lymbery, 2009). The very nature of social work and 'what a social worker is' has long been debated. This has made it difficult to ensure that educational curricula were appropriate and provided a sound foundation for practice. However, following on from the work of the Social Work Task Force (2009), recent important steps have been taken to resolve the debate, resulting in the introduction by the College of Social Work of the Professional Capabilities Framework (PCF) (CSW, 2012). This new framework provides detailed standards and expectations against which social workers can be assessed and sets out a vision of what 'being a social worker' entails not just at qualification, but at all stages of their careers. At the time of writing this second edition, the profession is in a period of transition, with the new PCF (CSW, 2012) gradually replacing the National Occupational Standards (TOPSS, 2002) as the benchmark standard for social workers. Newly qualified social workers entering the profession since September 2012 will be amongst the first to be assessed formally against the PCF during their Assessed and Supported Year in Employment (ASYE), with students on qualifying courses following on in September 2013.

The introduction of the PCF has been an important development in social work education, as it has helped educators and employers determine much more comprehensively what social workers need to know and what they need to be able to do to fulfil their roles. Rather than being a single set of standards, like the National Occupational Standards that they replace (TOPSS, 2002), the PCF is a comprehensive framework with standards specified across nine domains to reflect expectations within these domains at eight key points in a social worker's career. Thus the PCF gives the clearest message yet that social workers are expected to continue to learn and develop throughout their professional careers. Key stakeholders such as employers, service users and carers have been involved in the development of the standards and are expected to continue to play a central role in the development and management of social work education at all levels. This is to ensure that the practice developed through education is not only competent but also 'fit for purpose'. The professional registration of all social workers ensures that some continuing professional development is undertaken by all social workers and provides a system for 'policing' the maintenance of standards (CSW, 2012).

Qualifying social workers currently spend a minimum of 200 days in practice placements, which provide learners with opportunities to transfer learning from the classroom setting to practice and to experience direct work with service users to enable learners to develop practice competence (Furness and Gilligan, 2004). The practice- or work-based learning element of the qualifying degree crucially provides the opportunity to assess students' competence in practice, using the PCF (CSW, 2012) to benchmark performance. This theme of the central importance of practice competence continues beyond qualification and into the first year in employment during which all newly qualified social workers will be assessed against the PCF standards that have been developed for the ASYE (CSW, 2012).

The National Occupational Standards (TOPSS, 2002) were developed as a competence-based system of assessment and have been much criticised as a result. Placing too much emphasis on competence-based assessment has a number of inherent dangers (Doel, et al., 2002). Students can be 'competent' without being suited to being social workers because students tend to be driven by assessment and will develop skills in being able to complete assessment tasks (Singh, 2001). The whole process of learning can become reduced to a 'tick box' exercise, where both students and assessors drive forward a learning agenda aimed solely at meeting assessment criteria. The danger of this approach is that learning is superficial, with little development of deep understanding of issues or of how skills and knowledge can be transferred from one setting or one problem to another (Biggs, 1999; Barnett and Coate, 2005; Clapton, et al., 2006). Reflect on your own experiences of competence-based assessment. Do you agree with the idea that competence-based systems have their limitations?

From competence to capability

While the assessment of competence has historically been considered an important part of ensuring that social workers are fit for practice, it is by no means the whole story. Competences can be thought of as ingredients, such as those needed to make a cake. It is important when making a cake to have all the specified ingredients of sufficient or 'good enough' quality. But having the right ingredients of the right quality does not ensure that the finished cake will be good to eat or 'fit for purpose'. A cake is more than the sum of its ingredients. The way the ingredients are brought together, the level of the cook's understanding of complex issues, such as the impact of humidity on flour and of temperature on eggs will all determine how the cake turns out. Subtle differences in techniques used can make a huge difference to the finished product.

Similarly, a social worker may have demonstrated that they have all the right 'ingredients' (competences) and that they are all of the right standard, but it is not just the competences themselves but the way that these competences are brought together and applied in fast-evolving, demanding and complex practice situations that determine how effective the social worker will be within their role. They need to be vigilant and understand the impact of subtle differences in situations and in people. They need to be able to respond flexibly, adapting their approach to meet the specific needs of each individual service user and each context.

Juanita is a newly qualified social worker and is just starting her first job in a learning disabilities team. She passed her degree with a 2.1 and was successful in both her placements. One of the first tasks Juanita was given was to support Jonathan, a 20-year-old man with complex needs and limited verbal communication, to prepare for a review. Jonathan currently lives with Emma and David, his parents, who are very loving and protective towards him. At their first meeting, which took place at a day centre, Jonathan told Juanita that he was considering a move to a local supported housing

continued

project and seemed to be quite excited about the idea. Juanita understands the importance of working to empower Jonathan and spends some time with him talking about his needs and wishes. She accompanies him on a visit to the housing project and talks to him about what the move would mean to him and his family. She talks to his parents, who are broadly supportive of a move and appear keen to help Jonathan achieve more independence. Juanita is confident by the time they attend the review that she will be able to help Jonathan express his wishes and is equally confident that Jonathan knows what he wants to do. They have even role-played the meeting to help Jonathan prepare.

However, when the review starts it quickly becomes obvious that Jonathan is going to say that he is happy at home and does not want to move. Whatever Juanita does she cannot get Jonathan to repeat the conversations that they have had about the housing project. He says he enjoyed their day out to the project but is happy at home with his mum and dad.

At various points during her work with Jonathan, Juanita demonstrated her competence – she had done what she needed to 'tick the right boxes' – but despite this she had not fully understood Jonathan's perspective or the true complexity of the situation. How could she have worked more effectively with Jonathan to find out what he really did want to do? How does she need to develop further as a practitioner? Most people would say that what Juanita needs is more experience – but what is it about 'experience' that can make us more effective within our roles?

Measuring or assessing performance against individual competences can help us, as educators, make judgements about a learner's ability to fulfil their role as a social worker, but the demonstration of competence is only part of the overall picture of professional development. Competence alone is not enough to equip social workers to be effective professionals. If we are going to improve the way that social workers function – particularly in complex and challenging settings – we must look at structuring education at all levels and stages to ensure that the rest of the picture is put in place. The development and introduction of the PCF is the first stage in this process. But although the PCF is intended to move the thinking of social workers and their educators away from a competence-based approach to assessing practice, the road ahead is still full of potential dangers. Unless there are fundamental changes in the way that social workers are taught and assessed, the PCF could still fail to bring about any real change and simply become yet another competence-based assessment tool.

Social work education now needs to focus not just on the demonstration of practice competence but also on enabling social workers to understand how practice competence can be brought together as a cohesive whole and how the skills, knowledge and attributes needed to work in complex situations can be developed. Some describe this process of broader learning as the development of professional capability (Barnett and Coate, 2005) or of dynamic competence (Manor, 2000, cited in Doel, et al., 2002). And it is an understanding of the importance of this more complex picture of what makes an effective social worker that has driven forward the development of the Professional Capabilities Framework (CSW, 2012). Lester (1999, cited in Cooper, 2008) likens the transition from competence to capability to the move from map reader to map maker. When a practitioner is a 'map maker' they constantly monitor and revise the way that they understand and map the 'territory' that they are working in (people and contexts). Although they will always have to follow map-making rules, the old map can be amended or even torn up and replaced if circumstances change so much that a new inter-pretation and representation are required. By contrast, map readers are constrained in their practice and have to follow the map that has already been laid out by others. A social worker who is a 'map reader' is in danger of practice that is rigid, lacks creativity and is unresponsive to the needs of service users and carers. The map analogy is helpful because it provides us with a simple way of thinking about some important aspects of professional capability and the transi-tion that social workers need to make so as to ensure that they can function effectively within their complex roles.

Although historically there has been a strong focus on the measurement of practice compe-tence in social work learning, the development of professional capability has not been neglected by education policymakers. The QAAHE Benchmark Statement for Social Policy and Social Work (QAAHE, 2000), on which all social work programmes have been based, places a strong emphasis not only on the assessment of practice competence, but also on integrated learning aimed at developing critical reflexivity and problem-solving abilities that can be applied to practice. The Benchmark Statement stresses that one of the principal purposes of practice learning is to ensure that what have previously been considered to be 'academic skills and attributes' such as critical analysis, critical evaluation, problem-solving and dealing with uncertainty are transferred from the academic to the practice arena.

But the transfer of so-called academic skills is not automatic and may not happen at all – unless specific additional learning support is provided in the workplace (Moon, 1999). Students who are able to critically analyse a piece of research or solve complex theoretical problems in a university setting will not necessarily critically analyse their practice or the agency in which they are working. In a study of social work students, Ford, et al. (2005) showed that students' ability to be critical of their practice was fairly limited at the point of qualification and still needed further development. More evidence of the failure to transfer academic learning into practice comes from outside social work, where studies of business students have shown that teaching thinking skills within formal education does not necessarily enable learners to deal with com-plex problems in work situations (Smith, 2003). In a recent review of social work education, Clapton, et al. (2006) concluded that the gap between academic and practice elements of education was increasing, making it even less likely that a transfer of learning would occur.

So we can see that social work students need support in their practice placements not just to demonstrate competence but also to transfer and further develop academic skills which will enable them to develop their professional capability. Furthermore, on initial qualification this development is far from complete and during the newly qualified and post-qualification per-iods, social workers need to continue to build on the skills and attributes which enhance their effectiveness within their professional roles. We will look in more detail in the next section at how this can be achieved and how practice educators can support learners to develop their professional capability as well as assess their competence.

Developing professional capability through work-based learning

What skills and attributes make up professional capability?

As we have already established, it is important for professionals such as social workers to develop an appropriate set of competences. This will be made up of a critical understanding of a relevant knowledge base and a specific set of skills and will be underpinned by an appropriate professional value base. However, as we have indicated, there is an emerging consensus in the professional and education literature that these alone are not enough to ensure that professionals will be able to function effectively throughout their careers. Success in the workplace is dependent not just on the development of a fixed set of competences but on the development of a range of transferable skills and appropriate professional attributes which interlink to form professional capability (Eraut, 1994; Barnett and Coate, 2005).

RESEARCH SUMMARY 1.1

Skills and attributes that contribute to professional capability include adaptability, reflexivity, flexibility, creativity, critical analysis and evaluation, problem-solving, team working, critical thinking, self-reliance, critical self-awareness, open-mindedness and recognition of multiple perspectives, being able to deal with uncertainty and change, motivation to learn and develop, and the ability to learn to how to learn.

Learners who actively incorporate these skills in their practice will be effective career-long practitioners who can work independently, deal with complexity and embrace change because they will:

- *understand the need to keep their knowledge and skills up to date and recognise gaps in their existing capability;*
- *have the skills and motivation needed to update knowledge and skills independently;*
- *evaluate new learning and place it in the context of what is already known;*
- *understand how to adapt and transfer learning from one situation to another, ensuring that they can function effectively when faced with new situations;*
- *reflect critically on their own practice and the practice of others and use this for the purposes of learning and development;*
- *be able to articulate and critically evaluate their knowledge to make decision-making more systematic;*
- *be able to use critical thinking skills to solve problems and take responsibility for decision-making;*
- *be able to work effectively with others, recognising and valuing complementary skills and knowledge;*
- *have professional humility and be open to listening to the views of others;*
- *have a critical understanding of, and adherence to, an appropriate professional value base.*

Based on Barnett and Coate (2005)

---

ating the development of professional capability

tive professional educators (both academic and practice-based) will need to ensure that
develop and support learning opportunities that enable learners to value and develop the
skills and attributes identified above. To do so, they will need to take a creative approach to
learning support and assessment which encourages the development of wider skills and
enables learners to become self-reliant, critical practitioners (Fraser and Matthews, 2008).
Although it is particularly important to get this right for qualifying social work students,
practice educators can also have an important role in ensuring that qualified social workers
are enabled to further develop their transferable skills through post-qualification and continuing professional development.

There are a number of models of professional capability that can help us think about how the
skills and attributes can be developed in social work learners.

Model 1: The three pillars of social work

Older concepts of social work practice (e.g. CCETSW, 1995) define professional capability in
terms of knowledge, skills and values, described by O'Hagan (1996) as the three pillars of
professional social work. The model suggested that professional development could be guided
by focusing on development in these three areas with learners. However, Cree, et al. (1998)
criticised this familiar model by saying that it was misleading to conceptualise social work in
this way, as the simple model did not stress the importance of the interactions between the
three elements. They pointed out that skills and knowledge cannot be viewed as separate
entities as the two are inextricably linked. It is difficult to conceive of a situation in which it
would be possible to act skilfully without relevant knowledge to inform and guide action.
Furthermore, it would be equally misguided to think of values in isolation, as in most situations
values influence the way that social workers interpret knowledge and the way in which skills are
used in practice. The implication of Cree et al.'s critique is that social work learners must not
only focus on skills, knowledge and values but also understand the way that the three aspects
of professional practice interact.

Model 2: Biggs's model

Writing more generally about professional rather than social work development, Biggs (2003)
took the same fundamental building blocks of knowledge, skills and values but did address the
importance of the interaction between the elements. He proposed that professionals need to
develop 'functioning knowledge', which he considered to be made up of three essential components:

- knowing about things (knowledge);
- knowing how to do things (skills);
- knowing when to do these things and why (knowledge, skills and values brought
  together).

He went on to say that functioning knowledge can be developed only through 'deep learning'
(see Part Two) which enables learners to understand how the three types of knowledge interact
with each other within a real world setting.

In your role as practice educator you can use this model to help you think about the way you
structure and support learning for students and other learners and how you can assess their

practice more holistically. It stresses the importance of knowing about things – supporting the student to develop a relevant knowledge base (knowledge about the service user, the context, services and resources available, relevant policies and legislation and theories which would help the student understand the service user or context more effectively). It also highlights the importance of knowing how to do things (knowledge and understanding of social work models and approaches, skills such as communication, interviewing, assessment as well as organisational procedures). Possibly the most important element in this model is the last element – 'knowing when to do things and why'. Understanding when to do things and why demands a complex and critical approach to practice. The model helps educators understand the importance of enabling the development of a critical approach (e.g. capability) rather than discrete pieces of knowledge and skills (e.g. competence). We will move on to explore some of the ways that you can support the development of a critical approach to practice in later parts of the book.

Model 3: The Barnett and Coate model

Barnett and Coate (2005) also offer a model that can help us to understand how we can enable professional learning in practice. As with the previous models we have considered, this model incorporates three broad areas (or domains) for development and, again, the familiar domains of knowledge, skills and values can be recognised – labelled this time as knowing, acting and being. Like the second model, the Barnett and Coate model strongly stresses the importance of considering these as interlinking – not separate – domains.

More about knowing   Most people agree that social workers need to have a sound working knowledge of current legislation and an understanding of the theory and research that underpin and inform their practice (Thompson, 2005). Barnett and Coate (2005) agree that a relevant knowledge base is an important foundation for practice but suggest that it is not the knowledge itself that is the most important aspect of being a capable professional. After all, having knowledge does not mean that you know how to evaluate or apply it, and knowledge without these transferable skills is at best worthless, and can at worst be dangerous. Barnett and Coate (2005) therefore believe that professionals need to develop skills in knowledge acquisition, analysis, evaluation and understanding of how to critically apply knowledge to practice situations.

This makes sense for three reasons.

- A great deal of what is considered today to be a relevant knowledge base will shortly be out of date and will be superseded (legislation, policies, theories and research). Social workers need to keep their knowledge base under review and update it regularly.

- We live in a world where information is readily accessible and it is no longer so important to hold knowledge in our heads. It is more important that we know what information is available to us and how to access it effectively and efficiently. This means that we can access the 'best' information available to us at any given time.

- In social work there is rarely one right answer or one way to solve a problem – social workers therefore need to be able to think critically about the knowledge they access, to understand that there will be often multiple sources of information that may be contradictory or conflicting, and to be open-minded about evidence that goes against their existing beliefs.

There are some direct implications for practice educators in this model because to support learners effectively we need to have the confidence and skills to facilitate the development of research skills, critical analysis and critical evaluation. We also need to be able to model a critical stance within our own practice in order to provide learners with a real-life example of the value of critical practice and how it can be achieved (Moon, 1999). We need to facilitate learning experiences that maximise the opportunities for learners to explore, analyse and apply their knowledge in a variety of contexts and not just learn information by rote. Part Two will provide some ideas for how this can be achieved.

CASE STUDY 1.2

Germaine is a drug and alcohol worker based in a community project and is an experienced practice educator. He is currently working with James, a final-year social work student. In a supervision session Germaine suggests that James reads about various approaches that could be used with the young people in the project and recommends some relevant recent research papers. He asks James to select two contrasting approaches and bring notes to the next supervision session about what he understands to be the strengths and weaknesses of the two approaches. In the supervision session Germaine helps James to deepen his critical understanding of the approaches by encouraging him to analyse and evaluate them in depth, making the learning more relevant by thinking about how they could be used with specific service users.

More about acting   This domain focuses on the way that professionals 'act' in practice situations and on the underlying skills and attributes that guide and define their actions. Social workers need to practise skilfully and, of course, need to develop a basic range of practice skills that will enable them to work with service users and their carers as well as with other professionals. However, Barnett and Coate (2005) suggest that it is not the development of specific skills *per se* that demonstrates capability but rather the ability to learn new skills effectively, to evaluate skills and understand how and when to apply those skills in practice.

So, rather than focusing on just teaching social work learners specific practice skills, their education and training should enable them to develop the ability to learn new skills, critically appraise and evaluate their own actions and to be adaptable enough to 'act' in a flexible manner in a wide range of circumstances.

When designing learning activities for students and other learners you therefore need to incorporate activities that encourage learners to critically analyse and evaluate the skills they use in their practice and provide opportunities to explore alternative approaches wherever possible. This will help reinforce learners' understanding that there is usually more than one possible approach to working in a complex situation and that there is often no 'right approach' or 'right way' to do something in professional practice. Activities that help learners to identify and analyse the sometimes subtle differences between apparently similar service users are good learning experiences (case studies can be a good way of doing this). As with support for development in the knowing domain, practice educators can play a key role through modelling a critical approach to practice and by ensuring that learners are supported to critically reflect on the skills that they are using.

The 'being' domain is central to the Barnett and Coate (2005) model and is the area in which it varies most significantly from other models of professional development. According to Barnett and Coate (2005), learning in this domain, which includes developing a sense of self-awareness, self-confidence and development as reflective practitioners, is fundamental to effective professional performance in a modern world. Fundamental to development in this area is the integration of both personal and professional values into approaches to practice. (An exercise in the next section of this chapter will encourage you to begin to look at your own value base with regard to enabling others.)

Again, the model has clear applicability in work-based learning situations, underlining the importance of maximising opportunities for the development of professional reflexivity, professional self-awareness, the confidence to work independently and take responsibility for one's own practice and one's own professional development. The development of the attributes included in this domain is crucial to success in social work and other allied professions. It is therefore important that we consider ways in which we can support social work learners at all stages of their careers to develop within this domain. You will find ideas for how you can support learning in the 'being' domain in all of the following parts of the book.

Barnett and Coate (2005) represent these three domains as overlapping circles. This model, as with earlier models, reinforces the importance of developing an integrated capability across all three domains to produce professional capability. It follows that learning and teaching should be designed to ensure that integration takes place between all three domains, and that educators help learners to make links between their experiences. With work-based experiential learning there is the potential for this to happen because in real-life situations learning cannot be separated into neat compartments. As we will see later, an essential component of work-based learning is reflection on 'whole practice experiences' and many theorists believe that it is through the act of critical reflection on experience that professional learning is achieved (Eraut, 1994; Moon, 1999; Fraser and Matthews, 2008; Beddoe, 2009).

The Professional Capabilities Framework (CSW, 2012)

The models that we have just explored are very useful as they can help us to understand the principles that underpin the concept of professional capability. However, they don't provide us with a specific tool that can be applied to guide development and assess practice capability in the social work profession. Since autumn 2012 the College of Social Work has promoted the introduction of the Professional Capabilities Framework (PCF). This framework was initially developed by the Social Work Reform Board (SWRB, 2010) and is intended to provide a capability benchmark against which social workers at all stages of their careers can be measured. It will progressively replace the National Occupational Standards (TOPSS, 2002) as an assessment framework for qualifying students and newly qualified social workers.

Domains

The PCF has nine domains within it:

- professionalism;
- values and ethics;
- diversity;
- rights, justice and economic wellbeing;
- knowledge;
- critical reflection and analysis;
- intervention and skills;

- contexts and organisations;
- professional leadership.

Levels

The PCF is divided into nine levels. The levels relate to the complexity of work that someone with those capabilities would be able to manage. The nine levels are:

- point of entry to social work programme;
- point of assessment of readiness for direct practice;
- end of first placement;
- end of last placement/completion of qualifying programme;
- end of Assessed and Supported Year in Employment (ASYE);
- in the social work role;
- experienced social worker;
- advanced level practitioner;
- strategic level practitioner.

Further detailed information about the PCF is available from the College of Social Work website www.collegeofsocialwork.org/pcf.

The use of the PCF for assessment purposes will be explored further in Part Three of this book.

Links between the PCF and the Health and Care Professions Council (HCPC) Standards of Proficiency for Social Work

As part of their regulatory function the HCPC has produced a set of Standards for Proficiency for Social Work (HCPC, 2012). These set out threshold standards for what social workers need to know, understand and be able to do at the point of qualification. Alongside these standards the HCPC also specifies standards for conduct performance and ethics. All social workers must meet these minimum standards to stay on the Social Work Register. The HCPC standards have been mapped against the PCF standards at the end of the final placement and although there are differences in language, the overall expectations are the same. Practice educators can therefore be confident that any practitioner who meets the PCF at this level or above will also be meeting the HCPC Standards of Proficiency.

The role of the practice educator in supporting work-based learning

We have now established that in order to practise effectively as a professional social worker it is important not only to be competent but also to practise in a way that is professionally capable. We have explored the attributes and approaches to practice that capability involves and now we are now going look some more at the practice educator's roles and responsibilities in supporting learners not just to develop and demonstrate competence but also to help them with their journey towards capability. The themes identified in this section will be developed more fully in subsequent sections in which we will provide more practical guidance on how to fulfil the roles and responsibilities identified here.

Although traditionally practice educators have been thought of as the people who are responsible for student social workers, the specific skills and attributes that you develop as a practice educator will equip you to support learners in different contexts and at all stages of their careers. Here are just a few examples of how you could use your skills and knowledge to support learning in the workplace.

- Managing, enabling and assessing social work students in practice placements.
- Supporting, enabling and assessing newly qualified social workers during their first year of practice.
- Supporting and assessing colleagues undertaking post-qualifying awards.
- Supporting and assessing unqualified staff undertaking work-based learning.
- Organising and supporting the induction of new staff.
- Mentoring or coaching colleagues.
- Providing support with continuing professional development.
- Providing supervision.
- Organising team-based learning events.

Before we go on to look at what other people think the role of a practice educator is, it will be useful for you to complete the following activity. This will help you to reflect on your experiences of work-based learning to enable you to draw on both good and bad experiences and guide your future practice.

ACTIVITY *1.5*

What do you consider to be the main roles and responsibilities of a practice educator for a social work student?
Think in terms of:
(a) managing and co-ordinating learning;
(b) enabling learning (teaching);
(c) assessment.
Would you have come up with a different list for a practice educator working with a newly qualified social worker or mentoring a colleague? What are the differences and why?

Comment

More detail about your roles and responsibilities as a practice educator will be found in the course materials provided by the university that places students in your workplace.

The Practice Educator Professional Standards (PEPS) (CSW, 2012) have been developed to describe the responsibilities of a practice educator and has been divided in the following domains.

- Domain A: Organise opportunities for the demonstration of assessed competence in practice.
- Domain B: Enable learning and professional development in practice.
- Domain C: Manage the assessment of learners in practice.

- Domain D: Effective continuing performance as a practice educator.

Each domain is described in full at the beginning of Parts One to Four and we will see that a whole range of skills, knowledge and attributes are considered relevant to the role. The way you can meet the expectations of these domains will be considered in detail as we explore how you can manage learning in the workplace and provide learners with opportunities to demonstrate competence, how you can enable and assess learning and how you can ensure that you critically reflect on your own practice and continue to perform effectively as a practice educator.

REFLECTION POINT

As a social worker, your values are an important element of your practice and of your professional capability. Values will influence all your decisions and actions and will be just as important in your work with learners as they are in other areas of your professional practice. Thinking critically about your value base will help you to understand how your values will impact on your practice. Consider your values with respect to facilitating and assessing practice and think about how these values differ from your more familiar professional value base. Why do you think you hold these particular values? Can you link them to any specific experiences that you have had as a learner or as a practice educator? How do you think that your values will guide and influence your practice with learners?

These are the GSCC (2002) values for practice educators that have been incorporated into the PEPS (CSW, 2012).

- Identify and question their own values and prejudices, the use of authority and power in the assessment relationship, and recognise and act upon the implications for their assessment practice.

- Update themselves on best practice in assessment and research on adult learning and apply this knowledge in promoting the rights and choices of learners and managing the assessment process.

- Respect and value the uniqueness and diversity of learners and recognise and build on strengths, and take into account individual learning styles and preferred assessment methods.

- Accept and respect learners' circumstances and understand how they impact on the assessment process.

- Assess in a manner that does not stigmatise or disadvantage individuals and assures equality of opportunity. Show applied knowledge and understanding of the significance of: poverty, racism, ill health and disability, gender, social class and sexual orientation in managing the assessment process.

- Recognise and work to prevent unjustifiable discrimination and disadvantage in all aspects of the assessment process, and counter any unjustifiable discrimination in the ways that are appropriate to their situation and role.

- Take responsibility for the quality of their work and ensure that it is monitored and appraised; critically reflect on their own practice and identify development needs in order to improve their own performance, raise standards and contribute to the learning and development of others.

As can be seen, these values advocate certain approaches and processes for the task of enabling learning by ensuring practice is of a high professional standard, and that it is ethical, non-discriminatory and fair.

ACTIVITY *1.6*

Write a few words on the skills, knowledge and personal qualities you are bringing to the role of practice educator.

Remember that skills and knowledge are often transferable from other areas of your life. For instance, you may never have had experience of supporting adults to learn in a formal setting but you may know that you are good at breaking tasks down into simple-to-understand steps and can explain them to people.

Think about how you will need to build on these skills, knowledge and attributes as you become more experienced within the role. What new knowledge will you need? What skills will you need to develop? Where will values fit in? Remember that it is not always possible to draw clear distinctions between knowledge, values and skills.

It may help you to draw a mind map (or other representation, table, list, pictures, etc.) of the things that you think you need to learn to help you become a more effective practice educator. Include your ideas about how this learning will be achieved (e.g. 'I need to know more about how adults learn. I will learn about this by reading, attending workshops and by reflecting on my experience of working with a learner').

Comment

This exercise will provide you with an analysis of your existing skills, knowledge and values and will encourage you to think about areas for further development. This could form the basis for an action plan.

C H A P T E R S U M M A R Y

- Learning is taking place in every workplace almost all of the time – each time something new is encountered there is the potential to learn from it.

- If professional education and frameworks for continuing development are to be fit for purpose, they must ensure that they promote the development of skills and attributes that will enable professionals such as social workers to be effective in their role in this rapidly evolving and complex work climate.

- Effective work-based education should focus not only on learning and assessment for the demonstration of practice competence but also on bringing the competences together into a cohesive whole, which some describe as the development of professional capability or dynamic competence.

- Success in the workplace is dependent not just on the development of a fixed set of competences but critically on the development of a range of transferable skills and appropriate professional attributes that interlink to form professional capability.

- As a social worker, your values will be important in guiding your approach to the task of supporting and assessing learning in practice.

FURTHER READING

Barnett, R and Coate, K (2005) *Engaging the curriculum in higher education*. Maidenhead: Open University Press.
An interesting, if academic, text for those interested in reading more about these authors' model of being, knowing and acting.

Gould, N and Baldwin, M (eds) (2004) *Social work, critical reflection and the learning organisation*. Aldershot: Ashgate. Chapter 8.
An interesting book which explores the importance of critical reflection in social work and the links between critical reflection and the creation of learning organisations.

Nixon, S and Murr, A (2006) Practice learning and the development of professional practice. *Social Work Education*, 25 (8), 798–811.
An interesting exploration of social work learning in the current challenging climate.

Walker, J, Crawford, K and Parker, J (2008) *Practice education in social work: A handbook for practice teachers, assessors and educators*. Exeter: Learning Matters.
A theoretical and practical guide to the role of the practice educator, helping to develop skills and practice.

Part One
Domain A: Organise opportunities for the demonstration of assessed competence in practice

Meeting the requirements of the Practice Educator Professional Standards (CSW, 2012)

The material in this part links to the following domain standards.

Domain A: Organise opportunities for the demonstration of assessed competence in practice

1. Take responsibility for creating a physical and learning environment conducive to the demonstration of assessed competence.

2. Devise an induction programme for social work students that takes into account a learner's needs and their previous experience.

3. Negotiate with all participants in the workplace, including service users and carers, the appropriate learning opportunities and the necessary resources to enable the demonstration of practice competence.

4. Work openly and co-operatively with learners, their line managers, workplace colleagues, other professionals, and service users and carers, in the planning of key activities at all stages of learning and assessment.

5. Co-ordinate the work of all contributors. Ensure they are fully briefed, understand their roles and provide them with feedback.

6. Complete an audit and provide feedback on practice learning opportunity in line with the Quality Assurance for Practice Learning framework.

7. Monitor, critically evaluate and report on the continuing suitability of the work environment, learning opportunities, and resources. Take appropriate action to address any shortcomings and optimise learning and assessment.

8. Contribute to the learning and development of the agency as a training organisation. Help to review and improve its provision, policies and procedures and identify barriers for learners.

Introduction to Domain A

When I organised my son's eighth birthday party I had everything planned down to the last detail. I researched and selected party games, shopped around for interesting prizes and worried about which children to invite. I considered and then reconsidered all sorts of different food before finally settling on what I hoped would be the perfect menu – a menu that would have something for everyone, would not give too much of a sugar rush or lead to any nasty allergic reactions. In the run-up to the party I had 'to do' lists pinned all over my kitchen and every spare moment was filled with activities related to the organisation of those two short hours. On the big day it was worth it. Although I knew of course that things could still go wrong, the careful planning made me more confident and provided me with a range of plan Bs for times when the plan As didn't quite work out. So, for instance, when I discovered during a game of Pass the Parcel that I had miscalculated the number of layers and did not quite have enough prizes to go around, I had a bag of spare prizes to hand and was able to placate the child who had missed his turn. Later, when another boy fell over and cut his knee in the garden, the first aid kit was waiting by the back door and I could stick a plaster on the cut with minimum fuss.

Although you may feel that my approach to my son's birthday says more about my personality than about planning and organisation in general, there are some important points that can be drawn from my experience. Most people would agree that when outcomes matter good planning and organisation are important. We can all think about times when poor planning and preparation has led to disappointing results in both our personal and professional lives. For me and for my son the outcome of the party was very important and I was fortunate because I could choose to prioritise my time to invest in planning and preparation. In work situations we do not always have the luxury of time or the autonomy to choose how we spend it. We have many competing priorities and very often planning thoroughly for learning opportunities quite understandably comes low down on our list of things to do.

In Part One (Domain A) we will be thinking about planning and organising learning experiences for social work students on practice placements. These students will be spending between 70 and 100 days in your workplace and for the student, the service users, you and your team, the outcomes of the time they spend matter a great deal. However, in our experience, less time is sometimes spent planning and organising student placements than I spent planning and organising my son's two-hour-long birthday party. When planning is skimped, things commonly go wrong – students can struggle or even fail to meet their objectives, service users can be disadvantaged or even harmed and problems can arise within teams or within the wider organisation. Because the outcomes of social work placements matter and the consequences of poor planning and organisation have such far-reaching and serious consequences, workplace learning is not something that can be left to chance (Shardlow and Doel, 1996). It is therefore important that practice educators are able to spend time planning placements before they happen and have sufficient time and resources to work with learners to ensure that the learning experience is effectively organised from beginning to end.

Part One will provide you with the opportunity to think critically about the way that learning should be planned and organised in the workplace. It will also enable you to explore a range of organisational strategies that you can use in your work as a practice educator. Most of the examples used relate to social work students but many of the principles underpinning the examples can be applied to other learners such as newly qualified social workers or people undertaking continuing professional development.

Part One builds on the key themes introduced in Chapter 1 and looks at how you can organise and manage learning to ensure both the demonstration of competence and the development of professional capability. We will show that the way that learning is managed can have a significant impact on learning outcomes and that some management strategies are more likely than others to support the development of capability.

If you think back to Chapter 1, you will remember that Barnett and Coate (2005) suggest an important part of being a capable professional is having the ability to be an independent and self-motivated learner. This is of fundamental importance to social workers who need to be able to manage their own learning as part of their core professional role (CSW, 2012). However, it is worth bearing in mind that this is not something that comes naturally to everyone and some will need more support and guidance than others to begin to learn independently. We will therefore, explore ways that learners can be encouraged and enabled to take responsibility for managing their own learning within work-based learning experiences, using strategies that take into account individual needs.

Although the majority of work-based learning experiences go well, a small minority of learners and their practice educators will experience difficulties. This part of the book will look at some of the problems that can arise in work-based learning settings and at what you can do when things begin to go wrong. We will consider strategies that you can adopt to help you support and manage learners who are not meeting their objectives and are in danger of failing. These themes will be further developed in Parts Two and Three in which we will be looking more specifically at supporting marginal and failing students with learning and assessment.

Part One is divided into three chapters: 2, 3 and 4. Chapter 2 provides an introduction to the issues covered within Part One and links back to Chapter 1. We look at some of the reasons why it is important to encourage learners to take some or all of the responsibility for planning and organising their own learning. We make links to adult learning principles to show why this is important and to emphasise the key role of the partnership between the learner and the practice educator in the learning process. At the end of the Chapter 2 we identify seven key elements of planning and organising work-based learning. In Chapter 3 we move on to explore the first of these elements, effective planning and preparation, in more detail. Chapter 4 covers the remaining six elements.

Chapter 2

Planning and organising learning: A partnership approach

Before we look at some of the reasons why it is important to encourage learners to take some or all of the responsibility for planning and organising their own learning, we begin with a case study and an activity which will start you thinking about planning and organising learning from a learner's perspective.

Comment

In answering these questions try to put yourself into Beate's shoes and imagine how you would feel. To extend the activity and take a more critical approach, you could give Beate two contrasting characters traits (confident and anxious?) and see if you think this would make a difference to how she would react to the situation.

Devise a concrete action plan which would give some immediate structure to the placement and provide Beate with a chance to talk about how her first day had made her feel.

(N.B. There will be no single right approach to this activity.)

Who should plan and organise work-based learning?

In Chapter 1 we introduced the idea that social work learners should be encouraged and supported to take responsibility for managing their own learning, as the ability to do so is fundamental to their development as effective professionals. The Professional Capabilities Framework includes the ability to recognise and respond to one's own learning needs within the professionalism domain, with all social workers from the point of qualification onwards expected to be able to take responsibility for aspects of their own learning. However, this is not the only justification for you to work in this way and we are now going to look at some of the other reasons why encouraging learners to take some or all of the responsibility for their own learning is generally considered to be a good idea.

Historically, learning theories did not distinguish between childhood and adult learning but in 1980 Malcolm Knowles began a long-running debate by claiming that adult learners have some distinct characteristics and that learning outcomes can be improved when educators have an understanding of adults' learning needs and motivations. Knowles's (1980) claims formed the basis of his theory of 'andragogy' (the study of adult learning) and although many of his ideas are contentious and are now considered oversimplifications (because many of the characteristics he identified can apply equally well to some children and are by no means universal in adults), they are still thought to be a helpful starting point for any discussion about adult learning (Walker, et al., 2008).

RESEARCH SUMMARY 2.1

Andragogy – a theory of adult learning

Knowles developed the following 'principles' to describe adult learners.

Adult learners are autonomous and self-directed. *Adults have a different self-concept from children and most adults have reached a point of development where they see themselves as independent and capable of making their own decisions. If they come into a learning situation and have little or no autonomy, they may feel disempowered, and Knowles believed that this could reduce the quality of their learning.*

Adult learners have a wealth of knowledge and experience. *Adults approach education with an existing bank of knowledge and experience gained from educational, life and work experiences and this is a resource and foundation for future learning. Knowles believed that adults learn most effectively when they are encouraged to build on and develop their existing knowledge and when they are respected as people who already have skills and knowledge.*

Adult learners are goal-orientated. *Adults are most motivated to learn things that will help them achieve specific goals. Adults will therefore learn most effectively when the benefits of learning activities are specifically linked to the achievement of learning or life objectives.*

continued

Adult learners are relevancy-orientated. *Adults are most motivated to learn things they see an immediate use for; particularly learning which will help them 'solve a problem' that they have currently in their lives. Adults will therefore learn most effectively when clear links are made between what they are learning about in 'theory' and how they can use their new knowledge in practice.*
Based on Knowles (1980)

Implications for practice educators

There are some clear implications for practice educators in Knowles's (1980) ideas. If we accept his 'principles' as guidance on how to work with adult learners we can see that we will help adults to learn most effectively when we do the following.

- encourage and support them to be active participants in their learning – for example, by setting some or all of their own learning objectives, selecting and designing their own learning experiences and by taking some responsibility for monitoring and assessing their own progress and achievements;

- form an 'adult to adult' partnership with them that fully takes into account, recognises and values their existing skills and knowledge and uses this as a basis for further learning and development;

- help them to understand how their learning experiences are linked to their learning needs and goals.

The first two principles are particularly relevant to managing and organising learning in the workplace and will have significant implications for the way that the relationship between the practice educator and learner is established and maintained. You will see how these principles are relevant at all stages of managing and organising learning experiences as Part 1 unfolds and you will be given opportunities to reflect how you can incorporate them into your practice. We will also look at some of the ideas put forward more recently by writers such as Prosser and Trigwell (1999), Biggs (2003) and Beddoe (2009) and consider how they have helped us to understand that the relationship between a learner, an educator and the learning context are more complex than andragogy (Knowles, 1980) suggests.

ACTIVITY *2.2*

Reflect on Knowles's principles for adult learning and consider how well they describe you as a learner. It may help you to answer the following questions.

- *Do you always learn most effectively when you are able to be in control of your own learning or can you think of times when you would prefer to be more directed by a 'teacher'?*

- *Do you think that it is important for a practice educator to find out about what a learner already knows? How does it feel to be a learner whose previous knowledge and skills are not taken into account by a teacher?*

Comment

This exercise will help you to begin to think about some of the reasons why Knowles's theory of andragogy (1980) is controversial. Most people find that the extent to which they want to manage their own learning varies from situation to situation and will be dependent on a number of complex interacting variables such as confidence levels, context, learning task, time pressures, etc.

Different learners, different contexts – different management approaches

Every adult learner and every learning situation is unique. We have already seen that encouraging adults to take an active responsibility for their own learning can enhance their learning outcomes (Knowles, 1980, 1990). In this chapter we will consider how the extent to which this is possible or even desirable will vary considerably from situation to situation.

REFLECTION POINT

Work-based learning is not the same as classroom learning because it occurs in complex situations that involve real service users whose welfare can be directly affected by the learner's actions. It is a situation where mistakes can have serious consequences and this can lead to high levels of uncertainty and anxiety in learners (Walker, et al., 2008; Doel, 2010). This anxiety can quite reasonably reduce the learner's inclination to take risks and increase their need for security and direct guidance (Prosser and Trigwell, 1999). Practice educators will also have some strong motivations to 'keep control' of work-based learning as they normally carry some level of responsibility for their learner's workload and will feel responsible for the success or failure of the learning experience. As a consequence they may be tempted to 'play it safe' and keep as much control as possible of the management of the learning experience. In this way they can be assured that the learner will learn what they need to know and they can demonstrate that they have done their job thoroughly and efficiently. This means that practice educators and learners need to balance the considerable educational benefits of encouraging the learner to take responsibility for their own learning with the risks and stresses involved in doing so.

When deciding how to divide responsibility for managing learning with a learner, it is worth asking yourself what is behind your decision and how your approach to risk has influenced your and your learner's thinking.

A number of factors need to be taken into account when decisions are reached on how responsibility for organising and managing learning is distributed between the practice educator and the learner. These factors include:

- characteristics of the learner (confidence, motivation, expectations, ability, etc.);
- prior experiences of the learner (personal, work, educational);
- stage that the learner has reached in the learning process (novice, near-qualified, post-qualified, etc.);
- nature of the learning objectives (fixed, e.g. PCF), determined by learner, determined by employer, clear or ambiguous, etc.);

- nature of the assessment process (fixed, e.g. format provided by university, negotiable, fully understood by the learner, etc.);
- nature of work involved (e.g. level of complexity, level of inter-professional, inter-agency work involved, etc.);
- nature of the learning context (e.g. good or poor culture learning for learning, support and resources available to the learner);
- level of responsibility the learner is taking for practice and the risks attached to the work they are undertaking;
- who is accountable for the learner's practice (learner, practice educator or other);
- what safeguards are in place to ensure quality of service to the learner and quality of the overall learning experience (e.g. supervision, monitoring and reviews);
- what resources the learner has the authority to access or mobilise – some things may have to be organised and managed by the practice educator or a manager with appropriate levels of authority.

CASE STUDY 2.2

Hope is a second-year student on a BA (Hons) social work course at Exbury University. She is a 22-year-old black woman who lives with her parents near the university. She has a good academic record and has told her practice educator in a pre-placement meeting that she is confident meeting new people, self-motivated and enjoys a challenge. Although this is her first placement she has had some experience of working as a volunteer in youth groups and does part-time work in a residential home for older people. She started her placement at The Grove, an independent drug and alcohol drop-in centre, two weeks ago.

Gavin, her 35-year-old white male practice educator, recently completed a practice educator programme and knew that he 'should' be encouraging Hope to take responsibility for her own learning. He therefore took what Hope had told him about her confidence levels into account and suggested that she took responsibility for organising and managing part of her induction programme. Hope enthusiastically agreed to do so and after a brief initial induction to the project she was given a list of visits to make to other agencies that had close links to The Grove. Gavin gave her some leaflets about the projects and suggested that she should make contact with the organisations and arrange visits during the first month of her placement. Although she was told that the visits would be useful, she was not really given much guidance on what her objectives for the visits should be.

After three weeks in the placement Hope had failed to arrange any visits. She told her practice educator that she had tried but that although she had left numerous messages for people, no one had returned her calls. This seemed unlikely as the practice educator was in regular telephone contact with several of the agencies and knew that they had a good record of returning calls. Hope still seemed confident and said she would keep trying to make contact. The practice educator sensed that she was becoming anxious about the situation and reflected that she probably needed more help than he initially thought with organising her induction.

ACTIVITY 2.3

What do you think is really happening in this case study? What factors are involved in Hope's failure to organise induction visits? What would you have done differently if you had been Hope's practice educator:

- *in the first supervision where you talked about induction;*
- *at the end of the first week in the placement;*
- *after three weeks?*

Comment

This activity will encourage you to think about how you will begin to judge how and when it is appropriate to encourage a learner to take some responsibility for managing their learning. You can use the questions set out above to help with your analysis. An area to focus on is the way that Gavin judged Hope's ability to manage her own learning – could he have asked some different questions to find out more? Maybe he could have asked Hope to give him some examples of previous situations when she had used similar skills?

In some situations practice educators will need to take a lead role in the organisation of the learning process, while in others the learner themselves can take some or all of this responsibility. The balance of responsibilities for managing learning can change over time as the learner grows in confidence, becomes more familiar with the learning context and is clearer on how they can meet their objectives. In a learning experience, such as a student placement, the learner would normally be expected to move from a position of early dependence towards greater independence over the course of the placement. You can help learners to become more independent by providing appropriate safe opportunities in which they can take responsibility for their learning along with support and encouragement to do so.

But it is sometimes not enough to provide opportunities, support and encouragement to learners, as some have never developed the underlying confidence, skills and attributes needed to take on this level of responsibility. Some learners, particularly those who are inexperienced or whose previous educational experiences have not required them to manage their own learning, may need help to develop their ability to manage time, prioritise tasks, problem-solve and research information as well as help to build self-confidence and motivation (Barnett and Coate, 2005). Support with the development of these underlying skills and attributes should not be seen as added extras or things which are outside the practice educator's remit. This is because these skills and attributes will not only improve their ability to manage their learning but are transferable to other areas of their professional practice and will enhance their more general professional capability, for example, in the PCF domains of professionalism and knowledge (CSW, 2012).

Student social workers and newly qualified social workers (NQSWs) commonly lack the confidence, skills, local knowledge and networks that they need to manage their own learning processes effectively and safely. They are also in situations which are likely to cause high levels of anxiety and it has been shown that in such circumstances people have a tendency to want more direct guidance and support (Prosser and Trigwell, 1999). It is therefore common for students and other people who are new to learning situations to initially need considerable help organising and managing their learning. Throwing people in at the deep end is rarely a good strategy and our own experience of setting up student placements has shown us that where this approach is adopted, placements often do not get off to a good start.

Not all learners need high levels of initial support with the management of their learning and experienced social workers undertaking post-qualifying education or continuous professional development based in their own workplace will often be able to take some or even all of the responsibility for organising their own learning experience. It is, however, worth remembering that even experienced professionals sometimes lack confidence in a new learning role. It is therefore important to not only understand what the 'learner' is like in their more familiar professional role, but also to know about their previous experiences as a learner and about their level of self-confidence and competence with regard to the specific learning they are under-taking (Prosser and Trigwell, 1999). It is only by developing a good understanding of the learner and the learner's context that it is possible to establish how much support the learner will want and need with organising and managing their learning in the workplace.

Getting to know the learner and working with the learner to reach joint decisions about important issues such as how their learning will be managed, will be achieved most effectively when there is a learning partnership between the learner and the practice educator. We will now look at how learning partnerships and other key objectives relating to effective work-based learning can be achieved.

The seven elements of organising work-based learning

Work-based learning by definition is taking place in a situation where learning is not the number one priority. In social work environments the needs of the service users and their carers will quite rightly take priority over the needs of learners. And so practice educators and learners will therefore be faced with a careful balancing act to ensure that:

- the needs of the learner are met;
- the learner can balance their learning with other aspects of their workload;
- all others within the work environment (service users, carers, colleagues, etc.) are considered, respected and not significantly disadvantaged as a result of the learning taking place.

These objectives can be achieved by considering the following seven key elements of organisation.

1. *Effective planning and preparation*
   Ensuring that the needs of the learner can be met, that the impact of the learning on others has been considered, appropriate resources can be made available and that the learning experience can be accommodated within the organisation.

2. *Setting clear expectations*
   Ensuring that all involved in the learning experience understand their respective roles and are clear about what is expected from them.

3. *Providing an effective learning environment*
   Attending to all aspects of the learning environment and ensuring where possible it is adapted to meet each learner's individual needs.

4. *Ensuring effective communication*
   Ensuring that good strategies and processes are in place to facilitate effective communication between all interested parties.

5. *Providing appropriate support and monitoring progress*
   Ensuring that all aspects of the learning experience are monitored and supervised adequately and that appropriate support is provided to the learner throughout the learning experience.

6. *Undertaking regular reviews*
   Ensuring that progress is formally reviewed at agreed intervals and that there are strategies in place to deal with any problems that may arise.

7. *Evaluating the learning experience*
   Ensuring that the learning experience is evaluated and that information received is used to feed into the planning process for future work-based learning.

We will now look at each of the above in more detail.

Chapter 3
Effective planning and preparation (Element 1)

Building sound foundations is a crucial part of providing an effective learning experience with overall success dependent, at least partly, on the quality of the planning and preparation that takes place (Shardlow and Doel, 1996; Walker, et al., 2008). Our experience of working with university-based social work programmes at both pre- and post-qualification levels supports this idea and has shown us that a significant number of the common problems associated with learning in the workplace can be attributed to failures in the planning and preparation stages.

Managing any form of work-based learning is a complex task (Grey, 2002) and, when learning experiences are organised at the last moment, there is often not enough time to ensure that adequate resources are in place to meet learners' needs. Last-minute placements for social work students are sometimes unavoidable, for instance when a planned placement falls through, but unless a great deal of extra care is taken, they can turn into poor experiences for both the learner and the organisation providing the placement. Even when learning takes place in a learner's own workplace, things can go wrong if time has not been taken to ensure that adequate planning and preparation are undertaken; for example, resources not available, no time for discussion of learning/personal reflection on learning/feedback, lack of workload relief.

Planning and preparation should ideally start at the moment you first consider the possibility of providing support for learning in your workplace; this could be a request from a local university for a placement, a discussion with a colleague about providing mentoring support or involvement with a NQSW. It should continue through the early stages of the learning process. The tasks involved in planning and preparation can usefully be broken down into the following stages (although not all will be needed for all forms of learning):

- making the decision to provide a learning opportunity;
- consulting with and involving your agency in planning and preparation;
- consulting with and involving the learner in planning and preparation;
- planning and organising an induction programme.

Working though each of the relevant stages in a systematic way will help you to ensure that sound foundations are put in place for work-based learning experiences. It is unlikely that this will be a linear process because you will probably find that you need to revisit and revise some of your early plans in light of information gained throughout the planning and preparation process. For instance, you will need to consult your colleagues and managers about the possibility of supporting a learner at a very early stage when you may not know much about the learner or their course. At a later stage you will need to go back to them again with any new information gained from talking to the learner in more detail.

We will now consider each of these planning and preparation stages in further detail.

Making the decision to provide a learning opportunity

The first stage of the planning and preparation process involves working with your team to decide whether a placement or other learning opportunity can reasonably be provided in your workplace at this time. It is important to include everyone who will have a role in the placement, as the presence of a learner will have an impact on team dynamics and possibly on individual team members' workloads.

Whether you and your team are new to supporting work-based learning or have some previous experience, it is worth analysing your current position to ensure that you make an appropriate decision. This decision can be considered to be made up of two parts. First, is it appropriate for you/your organisation to support a learner at this time? Second, is it possible to meet this particular learner's needs? Saying 'yes' to a learner when you or your organisation are not in a position to fully support them and provide the opportunities they require is likely to end in, at best, a disappointing experience for all involved and, at worst, setting up the learner to fail.

CASE STUDY 3.1

Exbury University approached Rosebank Day Centre and asked them if they could take a second-year social work student on a 70-day placement. The manager, Sandra, who is the only qualified practice educator at the day centre, knows that she will be going on maternity leave for the last three weeks of the placement and is still unsure who will be covering for her in her absence. However, the team really enjoys having students on placement and the service users have been asking when the next student is coming. The university really values the placement as it has always been well organised and evaluated positively by students.

Sandra decides that she will say 'yes' to the student, having negotiated with a colleague, Nathan, who is also an experienced practice educator and the manager of a nearby residential project. They have agreed to share the placement and the practice educator responsibilities between the two projects. Nathan will take over the placement for the last few weeks and Sandra will contribute to the final report before she goes on maternity leave. The University is very pleased with this arrangement as it means that a valued placement can go ahead.

ACTIVITY 3.1

What do you think of Sandra's compromise? What plans will Sandra and Nathan need to make to ensure that the joint placement runs smoothly? Who else do you think they should have consulted?

Comment

You need to think about this situation and think ahead to some of the things that could go wrong. This will help you plan to avoid problems. The case study does not mention consulting with either the student or staff at the two projects. Would you like to have involved them or do you think that their input was not needed at this stage?

In some situations, circumstances may dictate that there is no option but to say 'no' to the provision of a learning opportunity, but in others, even when circumstances are not ideal, it may be possible to make reasonable changes which ensure that the learner's needs can be met. To help you reach a decision, you should consider if the experiences you can offer within your workplace match the learners' needs (Doel, et al., 1996). It may be helpful to consider the following questions.

Questions to ask about your organisation.

- What impact will a learner have within the organisation – will we need to make any changes and do we have the necessary resources to meet an additional team member's needs?

- Could there be any negative consequences of the placement for service users and carers – can these be minimised or avoided?

- What learning opportunities can we provide? Can we link with any other agencies or organisations to extend the opportunities we can offer? Can any other workers within the organisation offer specialist opportunities? Do agency policies or procedures limit any opportunities that can be offered?

- What previous experience do we have of supporting learning in the workplace? What can we learn from that previous experience to help us in this situation?

- How will other people such as colleagues, service users and other professionals need to be involved and what is their attitude to involvement in supporting learning? What skills do they have? Do they have any development needs to support their involvement?

Questions about you as practice educator.

- Do I have the time, knowledge, skills, motivation and resources to support the learner? Will there need to be any organisational changes to support me in my role as practice educator (workload relief, extra training or support, supervision for my role as practice educator)?

Questions about the learner and their course.

- What will the learner need to gain from the learning opportunity?

- What do they already know? What can they already do? What previous experience have they had that is relevant to this workplace?

- Do they have specific learning needs, or any other additional needs, and can we meet these needs?

- What does the learner's course require from the learning opportunity? (Learning and assessment requirements, commitments required from the work-based practice educator, such as attendance at meetings, etc.)

- What support will the course offer to me as the practice educator?

You can use the information gained by answering these questions to help you reach a decision about whether or not to offer a placement. Remember that very few learning situations are perfect and you will almost certainly need to make some compromises to make the placement work. Decide what is essential, what is desirable and where there are difficulties; try looking creatively at whether problems can be solved.

Consulting with and involving your agency in planning and preparation

Once you have decided that you can provide a placement for a student or can support a learner such as an NQSW, you need to start work on planning the learning experience itself. It is important that you continue to involve key people from within your organisation such as line managers, colleagues, service users and carers because all of these people will have contact with the learner and may become involved in the learning and/or assessment process. You may also need to involve people from outside agencies if the learner will be working with them on a regular basis.

It is worth thinking about why and how you want other people to be involved before you open any discussions. By thinking things through in advance you will be much clearer about your objectives and will be more likely to succeed in achieving them.

Thinking creatively and involving service users and carers in planning can enhance learning opportunities but it is important to weigh up in advance how they can legitimately and appropriately be involved (Walker, et al., 2008). Service users and carers will almost certainly be asked to provide feedback on the learner's performance during the placement but may be able to make a larger contribution to the assessment process given appropriate support to do so. It may also be possible for them to be involved in teaching; for example, by helping learners to understand more about the service user's perspective, but thought must be given to how tokenism and exploitation can be avoided (you can find more ideas for involving service users and carers in assessment in Part Three).

Managers will also need to be included in the planning process as they need to understand the implications for practice educators in terms of workload and flexibility as this may mean that changes to work practices or support mechanisms are required. Thinking about what your needs are going to be and having an open discussion with your line manager about them at an early stage is really important because it may be difficult to make changes later. Don't assume that you will have workload relief or that your manager can provide you with support and guidance on your practice educator role unless you have checked this in advance.

You should also not assume that other people will feel positive about working with a learner or about contributing to a learning experience. Learners can bring extra work and disruption to a workplace; their presence can be challenging to staff because they bring new ideas and question established practice. Service users and carers may be concerned about working with a 'learner' rather than an experienced member of the team or may be anxious about meeting a new face. Experience with marginal and failing students in the past may have reinforced negative views and pressures of work may be forcing people to concentrate their energy on what they see as the core elements of their work. This will almost certainly not include involvement in learning.

However, despite the challenges that can come with supporting work-based learning many social workers do feel very positive about getting involved, recognising that a core part of their professional role is to support the development of others (CSW, 2012). Having learners in the workplace brings advantages – new ideas can be refreshing and energising and students can often undertake projects or 'added value' pieces of work that your team does not normally have the resources to complete. Service users and carers often enjoy working with learners because they feel that they get more time and attention as the learners have reduced caseloads. Some even positively enjoy helping the student to learn.

It is likely that your team, service users and carers will include people with both positive and negative views towards students and other learners. An important part of the planning process is to provide information and reassurance to everyone who will be involved and include them, where possible, in major decision-making. This will ensure that you take their views into account and that they understand what you are expecting from them if they agree to have an involvement in the learning process. Experience shows that it is difficult, if not impossible, to provide a good-quality learning experience within a workplace without the full co-operation of all involved, so investing time and energy in consulting and involving others is definitely worthwhile.

The following section will help you to think about who needs to be involved and how you can go about supporting and encouraging their involvement with all stages of the learner's experience in your workplace.

Consulting with and involving the learner in planning and preparation

In Chapter 2 we established the importance of the development of an effective learning partnership between the practice educator and the learner as a basis for a successful learning experience (Knowles, 1980). The foundations of this partnership need to be built during the planning and preparation stage.

In a social work placement the first point of contact (after there has been an agreement in principle about a placement) between student and practice educator will normally be a phone call or email to arrange an informal workplace visit. The purpose of this meeting is to spend a little time with the learner, beginning the process of getting to know them, finding out about their specific learning needs and exploring how these needs can be met in your workplace. It is best if the meeting takes place a few weeks before the start of the learning experience. This will provide sufficient time for both the learner and the practice educator to undertake any preparation that is agreed at the meeting. This type of meeting is particularly important when a learner is coming into a 'placement' from outside the team, but can also be valuable for people learning within their own work environment because their learning needs will often be different from their working needs.

As well as finding out about the learner, the meeting will also provide the opportunity for you to let them know about your expectations and give them information about you and your work environment. Although pre-placement meetings are usually fairly informal, planning will help to ensure that both you and the learner get the most out of the time you spend together. Drawing up an agenda will help give structure to the meeting and ensure that key issues are covered. Sharing this agenda with the learner before the meeting and encouraging them to add agenda items is a good idea as this gives you both a chance to prepare for the meeting and bring any relevant information on the day. Working in this way sends the learner a clear message that they will be expected to take an active role in their own learning and provides a good starting point for an effective learning partnership. It might also be a good idea to suggest that the student does a small amount of reading about your service user group or your service before they come – maybe you could send a link to a website that would be helpful. This will again send a message regarding your expectations about the student taking some responsibility for their learning – all but the most confident students would welcome some signposting to relevant materials; however, don't expect them to do too much at this stage.

Work-based learning brochures

How are students and other new learners going to find out about your organisation and about you as a practice educator?

People do not generally remember or understand large amounts of information provided verbally in early meetings so it is worth considering how you will ensure important details are provided, understood and remembered (Mullins, 2005). Doel, et al. (1996) encourage those responsible for managing learning in the workplace to provide clear, brief, jargon-free information for newcomers in the form of a brochure. They suggest that a brochure should contain information about the practice educator, the team in which the learning will take place and the agency as a whole, covering professional experience, specific knowledge, skills and experience of individuals within the team, previous experiences of supporting work-based learning and information, and information about the service users that the team works with.

Doel, et al. (1996) also suggest looking for creative and meaningful ways of conveying information to learners rather than the brochure being made up of questions and answers. This could include, for example, providing information in the form of descriptions of typical days, profiles of service users or examples of work undertaken by other learners. It may
continued

Work-based learning brochures *continued*

even be a good idea to ask current or past learners to contribute to the brochure because they will be able to provide the learners' perspective on what should be included.

Although this is a very good idea, it is worth considering that, as with any brochure, creation is not the end of the task. Information will need to be regularly updated and revised to ensure that an up-to-date picture of the organisation is presented at all times. Brochures, even in their simplest form, require an investment of time and effort. Involving other team members in the production of the brochure can spread the load as well as being a useful team-building exercise which will help people to feel involved in the provision of practice learning opportunities. To avoid spending time 're-creating the wheel', it is worth considering what resources you could draw on for inclusion in the brochure. This could include mission statements, leaflets about services, etc. It is also worth thinking about whether you can collaborate with other practice educators in your agency to pool general resources, possibly coming up with some sections of the brochure that can be used across the organisation with others specifically developed for each workplace. Working co-operatively in this way may also help build supportive relationships with other practice educators, which will be useful at every stage of supporting work-based learning.

ACTIVITY 3.2

One of the things that it is useful to include in a brochure for new learners is a profile of you as a practitioner and as a practice educator. This will help the learner find out about you, your particular areas of expertise, experience and interest.

Try writing a profile that you could give to a social work student or an NQSW joining your team. What will you include?

Comment

Different people take different approaches to writing a profile and will choose to include quite different information – there is no right or wrong approach. You need to think carefully about what information will be useful to the learner, what will help them see you as someone who will be able to support them in a positive and skilful way. As part of your deliberations you should consider where to place appropriate boundaries, as this will help you to think about what to include and what to leave out.

In my role as a practice educator I normally provide learners with a brief summary of information about myself and my work experience and also include some material in the profile about how I learn and how I approach new ideas, as I think this is a useful way to introduce these topics. I give basic outline information about my personal life including that I am a mother of teenaged children because I believe that this gives me a specific perspective on my work. Not everyone feels comfortable about sharing details of their private life and you will need to make you own decision about this. You need to think about power issues as part of sharing information with a student – do you expect them to share information with you that you wouldn't be prepared to share with them? If so, how will this affect your relationship?

Planning and organising an induction programme

The value of a good induction programme for any new person in a working environment is widely recognised and is a vital part of ensuring competence to practice (Mullins, 2005).

Most organisations that employ social workers will have some form of induction process for new employees in place. Some may also have a specific procedure for students on placements. From September 2012 all newly qualified social workers will undertake an Assessed and Supported Year in Employment (ASYE) (CSW, 2012) and this should mean that very specific packages of support and assessment are made available by their employers during their induction period and beyond. When you plan the induction of a student or a newly qualified social worker the first obvious step is to investigate the policies, procedures and resources available within your organisation. These will normally provide guidance and structure for induction but will usually need to be tailored to meet the needs of individual workers. Further useful resources relating to induction and the ASYE are available from Skills for Care and the Children's Workforce Development Council websites.

Induction involves the introduction of a new person to the culture and environment of an organisation and should include an introduction to its policies, practices and members of staff (Mullins, 2005). In a social work agency an important part of this induction includes an introduction to the service users and carers who engage with the service, including activities that enable the new person to begin to understand their perspective, needs and wishes. A properly planned and designed induction programme will provide reassurance, aid motivation and improve performance. The induction period for a new worker generally extends over the first few months of employment. Clearly, when a learner is on a relatively short placement or other similar brief learning experience, the induction period will be shortened and it is important that the programme is designed to take this into account. Although it may be useful to get some ideas from a standardised induction process used within your organisation, each learner's induction should be developed individually, taking into account their specific needs for learning and support.

Where possible, learners should be encouraged to identify their own needs and take some control over the management of the induction process in line with adult learning principles (Knowles, 1980). However, it is important to remember that people in new situations often feel anxious and don't know what they don't know. This difficulty, even for confident learners, with identifying exactly what they should be learning about in an unfamiliar organisation means that some clear advice and guidance will be required from you in your role as practice educator. It has been shown that students normally welcome support from a knowledgeable practice educator at this stage of their learning experience (Parker, 2006).

It is always worth remembering that people find it very difficult to absorb large amounts of information in a short space of time, particularly in new situations. Even though we know that this is the case, we may still have to fight ourselves in early supervision sessions because we feel that we need to make sure we have told the student everything they need to know. The design of the induction programme should allow for a staged approach to learning with an option for information to be revisited and reviewed (Mullins, 2005).

Induction plans

A written copy should be given to the student including times and locations of activities. People responsible for each element of the plan need to be clearly indentified with their contact details. The plan should include:

- *detailed plans for the first day to include orientation to building, initial introductions to your team, health and safety, parking, expenses, etc.;*
- *introductions to key people – maybe some pre-arranged meetings to discuss their role, etc.;*
- *shadowing opportunities – with you and with colleagues;*
- *visits to other agencies – not all at once at the beginning as the student needs to get to know your team before they can understand the wider context in which you work;*
- *essential training – e.g. computer systems, etc.;*
- *suggested reading – policies, procedures information about methods and approaches specific to your service, relevant research, etc.;*
- *reflection time – make sure you build this in to allow the student to think about and learn from their experiences;*
- *time with the practice educator.*

Based on Maclean and Lloyd (2008)

You may also wish to consider an induction checklist where you can tick things off as they are covered. You should think about how you ensure students have access to information that they will need during their induction and throughout their placement. Many practice educators put together induction folders containing key policies and procedures, information about the team, meeting dates etc. An induction folder can be used to complement a brochure such as the one described earlier and can be personalised for each individual student.

ACTIVITY 3.3

What would you need to include in an induction programme for a social work student on their final placement in your workplace? How will you stage the programme so that you ensure you don't give too much information at once? Could the responsibility for delivering induction be shared? How would you encourage the student to take some responsibility for the management of the induction programme?

Comment

Remember to include information about your workplace, policies, procedures, the community you serve, service users, your team, and other linked organisations, etc.

Chapter 4
Organising learning (Elements 2–7)

Element 2: Setting clear expectations

It is very important that everyone involved in a learning process has a shared understanding of what is expected from them (Knowles, 1990; Neary, 2000; Maclean and Lloyd, 2008). If there is any confusion or disagreement about expectations at the start of the learning experience it is likely that problems will develop. This could lead to difficulties with the achievement of learning objectives, reductions in the quality of service provision, problematic relationships with colleagues or a breakdown in the relationship between the learner and the practice educator.

CASE STUDY 4.1

David was a social work student undertaking his first placement in a small school for children with learning disabilities. Staff at the school provided support to the children at meal times and expected that David would do the same. This expectation had not been discussed at the pre-placement meeting or included in the learning contract. David did not see how helping with lunch met his learning needs and so decided to use lunchtime to catch up with his reflective recording. David's colleagues felt that he should be helping with lunch because chatting with children informally over a meal gave an insight into their perspectives and helped build and maintain relationships. When Janine, the practice educator, explained why she felt that it was important to get involved, David happily did so. He said he wished he had understood the value of this experience from the start of the placement as he felt that he had inadvertently put relationships with his colleagues and children at risk through his behaviour.

Before any learning experience begins there should be agreement about a number of issues, including:

- the learning objectives;
- the learner's individual learning needs;
- what learning opportunities will be provided;
- what resources will be required to support learning;
- what support will be provided to the learner (supervision/mentoring, etc.);
- assessment methods and criteria;
- practical arrangements such as working times, line management and sickness;
- procedures to follow when things go wrong.

A generally accepted way of formalising agreements about learning is through a contract. The term 'contract' is one with which most adults are familiar – we have employment contracts, contracts regarding housing and even occasionally contracts regarding personal arrangements such as partnership. Contracts are binding agreements for people to carry out specific behaviours, often within a specified timescale. Before signing any form of contract it is important that all of the key people fully understand the implications of the agreement and their role within it.

Learning contracts are documents drawn up by those involved in a learning experience (for students in work-based learning this is usually the practice educator, the on-site supervisor, if relevant, the learner and the tutor from the learner's college/university course). They specify what the learner will learn, how this will be achieved, what resources will be available and the criteria that will be used for measuring success (Neary, 2000). Encouraging the learner to be actively and meaningfully involved in the process is important (Knowles, 1990). But remember that contracts are often drawn up early in the learning process, at a time when learners may be feeling anxious and powerless. They may not want to admit weaknesses or expose a lack of understanding. It is therefore important that you in your role as practice educator work in close partnership with the learner ensuring that they are empowered to contribute meaningfully to the process and are confident enough to make their needs and wishes known.

Learning contracts are usually agreed at a meeting that takes place between key individuals before, or shortly after, the start of a learning experience and are a very important part of the overall learning process. The exact timing of the contract meeting is open to debate (Walker, et al., 2008). Some people believe that the contract should be drawn up before the start of the learning experience and others within the first few weeks of the placement. Both approaches have advantages and disadvantages. Contracts are most effective when they are used as 'working documents', which are reviewed and if necessary revised at regular intervals, helping to keep learners and practice educators focused on the agreed learning objectives and assessment targets. If used in this way, the timing of drawing up the contract is probably not that critical, as changes can be made within the first few weeks as and when they are needed.

When a contract has been drawn up, Neary (2000) suggests reviewing it before finalising it by considering the following questions:

- Are the learning objectives clear, understandable and realistic? Do they describe what the learner proposes to learn?
- Are there any other objectives that should be considered?
- Do the learning opportunities seem reasonable, appropriate and efficient ways of achieving objectives?
- Are there other opportunities that could be utilised?
- Are the assessment criteria and means of validating them clear, relevant and convincing?
- Could other evidence be sought?

Many learning programmes will have their own specified way of assessing and collecting evidence for work-based learning. The contract will therefore usually include some material that is specified and non-negotiable, such as competences to be met and certain requirements for assessment, together with material that can be individually negotiated to meet the needs of a learner and/or the agency. It is very important to familiarise yourself with any guidance and requirements provided by learning programmes, including pro-formas developed for learning contracts. Seek advice from the learner's tutor or placement co-ordinator if you have any doubts about what is required.

Although learning contracts are most commonly used for 'placements' and for the Assessed and Supported Year in Employment (ASYE) their value in other work-based learning situations,

such as within mentoring, peer support or other forms of learning like continuing p
development, should also be considered. Formalising agreements through contra
the interests of the learners and their workplaces and ensures that the needs and expec..
of both are clearly communicated.

Element 3: Providing an effective learning environment

Think about your own experiences of work-based learning. What do you particularly remember? What helped you to learn and what made learning difficult? Whenever we ask these questions on practice education courses we get a wide variety of answers but if we had to select the ones that are most commonly given, they would relate to the relationship with the practice educator. This anecdotal finding has been strongly supported by research findings based on social work and nursing practice learning (Lefevre, 2005; Parker, 2008; Smedley and Morey, 2010).

What you do and the way that you interact with the learner is probably the single most important thing that will influence the quality of a learner's experience but when practice educators are asked to list what a learning environment is made up of, they often completely forget that they themselves are a central part of it.

People do not learn in a vacuum. They learn within a context made up of many variables that interact in a complex way and uniquely impact on individuals and their learning processes (Marton, et al., 1984). Getting the learning environment right and ensuring that it supports and encourages appropriate learning is an important aspect of the overall management of a work-based learning experience. Knowles first introduced the concept of a 'learning environment' in 1970. In his early work he explored the importance of physical (warmth, comfort, resources, etc.) and psychological needs (safety, appropriate level of challenge, respect, being treated as an adult, etc.), concluding that when these were not met, adults' learning could be seriously impaired. We can all remember a time when we have sat in an overheated or freezing room and found it almost impossible to do anything but wish for the session to end. Simple things like being too hot or cold, not having a comfortable chair or a desk to write on can have a significant impact on learning. We also find it hard to learn when we don't feel safe or are anxious; we can get put off by challenges that we think are too hard or can be inclined not to try when we perceive tasks to be too easy. But the situation is not straightforward as there is interplay between the factors that make up the learning environment – people who are motivated learners are less likely to be affected by the room's temperature.

Knowles also looked at the impact of social and cultural aspects of the environment and showed that these were important and could also influence learning outcomes. Knowles (1990) believed that if a learner's needs were not met, the quality of learning would be reduced and that they may 'vote with their feet' and opt out.

The relationship with the practice educator, relationships with other people providing support to the learner and the general atmosphere within the workplace are all important parts of the learning environment (Ellison, 1994, cited Lefevre, 2005). Lefevre (2005) found that students valued practice educators who were supportive, friendly, relaxed, open and respectful, were available and ready to share ideas. Although the majority of students would agree that having a practice educator with these attributes would support effective learning, there is not universal agreement among learners about other aspects of the learning environment. It is therefore unwise to make assumptions about an individual's needs based on a generalised impression of what a 'good' learning environment is.

Research has clearly shown that individual learners have very different needs and different ways of prioritising those needs (Biggs, 1999). Furthermore, it is the way that the learner perceives the environment that is significant to their learning and not any absolute measure of what is provided for them (Ramsden, 1992; Prosser and Trigwell, 1999). It is quite possible for different learners to perceive the same environment in substantially different ways, influenced by factors such as their previous learning experiences, expectations, motivation to learn, approach to learning and personal values (Prosser and Trigwell, 1999).

So returning to the relationship with the practice educator, although most learners would say that having a 'good' relationship with their practice educator was important to their learning, Lefevre's research (2005) showed that each student interviewed used different words to describe what worked for them. What one student would perceive as cold and formal, another might interpret as professional and efficient.

CASE STUDY 4.2

James and Julie have both just started placements in the same social work team. The team works in a cramped and noisy office with insufficient desks and computers to go around. James finds the noise, bustle and lack of personal space very stressful. He finds it hard to concentrate, hates not knowing if he will have a desk to work at and would rate the office as a very poor learning environment. Julie by contrast loves the 'buzz' in the office and feels that she learns a lot by hearing other people work and being able to talk things over with colleagues. She would rate the learning environment as good, even though she sometimes has to share a desk or phone.

Talking to the learner to find out what is important to them individually will help you to plan a learning environment within your organisational and resource constraints that comes as close as possible to meeting their individual needs. It will also help you to develop a relationship with the learner that is appropriate and meets their needs.

A very important aspect of the learning environment is the degree of inclusivity that it offers. Tisdell (1995) said that a learning environment should:

- acknowledge that all individuals bring multiple perspectives as a result of gender, class, age, sexuality, etc.;
- recognise that learners' identification with social groups is multiple and complex;
- reflect the experiences of learners and value these as a basis for learning and assessment;
- acknowledge the power disparity between teacher and learner.

Learners who feel marginalised and disempowered will not have their psychological, social or cultural needs met and this is likely to have a negative impact on their learning (Knowles, 1990; Prosser and Trigwell, 1999). Parker (2008) found a clear relationship between the inappropriate use of power and a breakdown in placements for social work students.

Learners arriving in placements are particularly likely to feel disempowered and marginalised and it is an important part of a practice educator's role to work in partnership with others to create an inclusive, supportive learning environment that meets each individual learner's needs. However, it is not just learners new to a workplace who may feel this way. Experienced workers can be 'destabilised' by new learning and as a result may feel disempowered. For example, social workers on a post-qualification 'critical thinking' course frequently comment that the processes involved in developing their critical thinking skills lead to an initial loss of professional confidence. Furthermore, because employers and colleagues are not always ready for the challenges that can result in increased criticality, learners report feelings of dissonance and, in some cases, even marginalisation. Practice educators can support individual learners with these sorts of experiences and can also work with others to ensure that team members and managers are open to new ideas and appropriate challenges.

Getting to know and forming a supportive relationship with individual learners is an important part of ensuring that the environment provided is inclusive and empowering (Smedley and Morey, 2010). Discussing and valuing previous experience, acknowledging and discussing difference without sentimentalising it, together with challenging stereotypes and checking assumptions, all have an important role to play (Doel, et al., 1996). Some 'differences', such as physical disability or ethnic background, may be relatively visible while others, which may be of equal importance to learners, may be less obvious.

ACTIVITY 4.1

Here are some examples of different people. What specific preparations would you need to make to ensure that the learning environment was suitable for them? Would their circumstances mean that you would have to make any day-to-day changes within your work environment to ensure that their needs were met?

Michaela is a 46-year-old Croatian woman who came to the UK two years ago and is retraining as a social worker. Her spoken and written English are good, but she has limited experience of living in this country.

Jethro is a 23-year-old man with severe dyslexia. He uses a specialist computer programme to help him write and needs support with reading complex material.

Helena is a 33-year-old single mother with two children under the age of five. One of her children has a physical disability. The learning opportunity is within an adult team that provides services for adults with various disabilities.

Comment

The changes you will need to make will depend partially on your own individual work environment. All three people described above could thrive in a workplace but would need some adjustments. You need to take into account relevant legislation, e.g. the Disability Discrimination Act 1995 (DDA). This act makes it unlawful to discriminate against people with a disability in the workplace. It also places a responsibility on employers to make reasonable adjustments to meet the needs of people with disabilities. You should bear in mind that dyslexia and other similar disabilities are covered by the DDA.

The learning environment not only has an influence on the likelihood of the success or failure of work-based learning, it will also have an impact on the quality of the learning that takes place. Returning to one of the key themes of this book – the development of professional capability –

we can see that the learning environment provided can play an important role in determining whether learners simply demonstrate competence or are supported to develop their capability.

Thompson (2006) stressed the importance of creating a culture within workplaces that supports all individuals to learn and develop. The following list draws on some of Thompson's ideas. An effective learning environment will be one in which:

- people are open to considering different approaches;
- people have a desire to look at issues from a service user/carer perspective;
- mechanisms exist for seeking service user and carer feedback;
- there is a willingness to learn from experience and there is an environment that supports critical reflection;
- it is possible to learn through safe experimentation and explore new ways of working;
- there is an expectation that learning will be shared;
- there is enthusiasm for an evidence-based approach to practice;
- there is good communication across professional boundaries;
- opportunities exist for people to share ideas and express opinions.

The provision of an effective learning culture supports the development of professional capability because it encourages social workers at all stages of their development to be open to new learning and to take a more critical, evidence-based approach to their practice (Hafford Letchfield, et al., 2008).

Although practice educators obviously play an important role in the provision of a culture for learning, work-based learning is most effectively supported when a learning culture exists across the whole organisation (Senge, 1990). A recent study by Beddoe (2009) suggests that there is considerable doubt that organisation-wide cultures can exist in large social work agencies. This is because learning is often directed in a top-down way by senior managers (who tell people what they need to learn rather than basing learning strategies on service user needs and what workers want to learn) and also because current managerialist and blame cultures have low levels of tolerance for learning from mistakes.

On a more optimistic note however, Beddoe (2009) concluded that even when organisation-wide cultures did not effectively support learning at a team level, it was still possible to create an effective learning culture. As a practice educator with a specific interest and skills in work-based learning you can have a direct influence on how the team culture develops.

See Part Four for more information on how a culture for learning can be provided within the supervisory relationship.

Element 4: Ensuring effective communication

Few people would disagree that effective and open communication is critical to the success of work-based learning situations. Most of us can remember times when failures in communication have led to misunderstandings or breakdowns in information transfer. When this happens in situations where people are learning, the potential for serious consequences for all involved is very significant. Learners may not have their needs met, tasks may be completed incorrectly or not at all, and service users and carers may receive an incomplete or poor-quality service.

In this element we will explore some key aspects of communication within work-based learning situations.

Communication with the learner

The imbalance of power within the relationship will have an impact on ↳
between the practice educator and the learner (Shardlow and Doel, 1996; Parker, ₂↳
a student, the practice educator occupies an authority role and has the power to assess ↳
practice and ultimately will have a say in whether or not they qualify as a social worker. They
may also have the power to provide or limit access to resources and learning experiences and
can have an influence on the opinions of others in the team.

However 'good' the relationship that develops between the learner and the practice educator,
the learner will retain a degree of apprehension as a result of the power held by the practice
educator. Communicating openly about mistakes, uncertainties and concerns can be difficult
when the learner is aware that their overall performance is being judged. Learners may also be
reluctant to criticise or question the practice of the agency or the practice educator because
they may fear the consequences of such behaviour.

Awareness by both the learner and the practice educator of the impact of this power imbalance, together with open discussions about what this will mean in practice, can help to
mitigate these negative effects on communication. It is a good idea for the practice educator
to raise the issue of power right at the start of the relationship and to talk about how any
concerns the student may have can be allayed.

Communication between the practice educator and the university/ training provider

Good communication between those responsible for supporting learners in the workplace and
the learner's education/training provider helps to ensure that learning experiences run smoothly
and problems that arise are dealt with effectively. Both practice educators and programme
providers will need to take some responsibility for establishing and maintaining effective working relationships. You will need to make sure that where possible you attend meetings for
practice educators that are arranged by the university and carefully read all written material
that is provided relating to the placement. Don't assume that just because you worked with the
university in the previous year that systems and procedures will be the same. Before the
placement starts read the placement handbook and ask for clarification about anything that
you are uncertain of.

In a study which looked at communication between higher educational establishments and
employers, Kemp (2000) showed that creating a collaborative relationship between universities
and work-based learning providers was not just desirable but essential when learners were
studying for qualifications that required:

- substantial practical skills and an in-depth knowledge base;
- integration through reflection and underpinning values;
- validation by professional and academic authorities.

Furthermore, Kemp (2000) showed that the formation of an effective collaborative relationship
was not a simple or linear process. Her research indicated that two interdependent factors were
significant in the development of such relationships: shared values and open communication.
She found that collaborative working was successful when effective professional relationships
developed between staff in universities and in placement agencies, as this enabled direct
communication to take place between key individuals.

If a problem arises within the placement it will be much easier to deal with if you have already been in communication with a tutor or practice learning co-ordinator from the university.

Element 5: Providing appropriate support and monitoring progress

Monitoring the learning/assessment experience is an important part of ensuring quality in terms of learning outcomes, practice performance and the interface between the two. Although the assessment of learning and the achievement of learning objectives/competences is an important part of the monitoring process, practice educators do not just monitor learning opportunities to measure whether learning is 'on track' (assessment). The monitoring role undertaken by practice educators is much wider and encompasses all aspects of learning and the learning environment. This will involve asking a series of questions.

- Is the learner's practice good enough for the role they are undertaking – does it meet agency standards; is the learner's work of a high enough quality to meet service users' needs (protecting service users and the agency)?
- Are the learner's support needs being met (protecting the learning process)?
- Is the learner able to meet their learning objectives (protecting the learner)?
- Is the quality of the learning experience good enough (developing the agency)?

Practice educators have a number of methods at their disposal that can be used to check the progress of the learner and the overall process of the learning experience, including:

- formal supervision (or practice tutorials);
- informal supervision (working alongside learners);
- evaluations of the learner's written records/assignments/reflective records, etc.;
- formal observation of practice;
- feedback from colleagues, managers, service users and carers and the learners themselves.

It is likely that a combination of the above methods would be used to monitor the success of a work-based learning opportunity as this will ensure that a variety of different perspectives are taken into account and that the interests of all involved in the learning environment are considered.

The practice educator will play a key role in monitoring the learning experience, working in partnership with the learner to draw together and analyse the information gained from the process. However, where possible, the practice educator should encourage learners to be partly responsible for monitoring their own progress. They can do this by supporting them to self-assess and keep track of progress towards objectives. This can be done formally in supervision where learners can be asked to report back on and evaluate progress since the last session. Most university qualifying programmes now build in processes that encourage students to monitor their own progress with the achievement of the Professional Capabilities Framework (PCF).

For a more in-depth exploration of some of these methods for monitoring learning experiences, see Part Three.

Element 6: Undertaking regular reviews

Regular reviews are an essential part of the quality-assurance process for work-based learning, providing both practice educators and learners with an opportunity to check progress with the achievement of objectives. Reviews draw on information gained through the monitoring processes described above and ensure that, when required, action is taken to keep learning experiences on track. Learning contracts should be used within the review process to check that intended learning outcomes are being met and that all involved are meeting their commitments.

Most learning programmes will have formal points of review where there will be the opportunity to review the contract, review objectives, monitor progress and devise an action plan for the remainder of the learning experience. Social work degree courses usually have formal review points in the middle and at the end of each practice learning opportunity (as a minimum). The dates of these reviews are usually included in the learning contract to ensure that all involved in the placement know when they will take place and can prepare appropriately. Reviews are usually undertaken at a meeting, but may in some cases be paper exercises.

Where learners are not studying through a formal programme, it may be worth agreeing points at which reviews will be undertaken between the learner and the practice educator. This will ensure that progress is regularly reviewed and that plans are made to help learners with the achievement of their goals.

CASE STUDY 4.3

Jacob is half-way through his placement in a Looked After Children team. He has settled in well and has developed a good working relationship with Diana, his practice educator. Diana is aware that they are approaching the mid-point of the placement and to help Jacob prepare they go through the pro-forma that will be used at the mid-way meeting together. Diana encourages Jacob to take the lead, reflecting on and evaluating his progress to date. They refer to the records Jacob is completing for his portfolio together with supervision notes, feedback from service users and colleagues. Although there has been an ongoing dialogue about progress in supervision, Jacob finds this preparation session with Diana very reassuring as it enables him to get a real overview of his progress. They do, however, identify that there may be a problem evidencing the professional leadership domain of the PCF, and agree to bring this up at the mid-way meeting.

A week later Diana and Jacob meet with the tutor from the university to review Jacob's progress to date. At the meeting Jacob raises the issue of lack of evidence for the domain and Jacob, Diana and the tutor explore ways that evidence could be provided. Diana is able to offer a few suggestions and as part of the review a specific objective is set for Jacob to deliver a short training session within a team meeting.

What happens when something goes wrong?

Work-based learners will not always do well and problems can sometimes be identified through reviews that lead to them being considered to be 'failing' or in danger of 'failing' the placement. Although some problems are easily resolved, it is important that both practice educators and the learners are aware of the possibility of 'failure' right from the start of the learning experience. This may sound very negative (and clearly discussions about the possibility of 'failure' need to be handled with great sensitivity), but it is much more likely that problems will be addressed and resolved quickly when strategies for failure have been agreed at an early stage (Sharp and Danbury, 1999).

There are many reasons why a learner will fail to meet objectives within a learning situation, some of which are not within the direct control of the learner (Sharp and Danbury, 1999). Once a concern is raised it is important to work in partnership with the learner to establish the reasons for the difficulties that have arisen. The earlier that this is done, the more chance there will be that learners will be able to overcome their problems and reach the required standards.

Questions to ask when a placement begins to go wrong

1. *Was the placement well prepared and did everything that was planned take place, e.g. induction?*
2. *Was everyone clear about their role and what was expected of them? Did everyone fulfil their role?*
3. *Was the learning agreement clear and was the learner actively involved in negotiating the agreement? Have there been opportunities to revise the agreement?*
4. *Was the assessment fair and transparent? Did the learner understand the assessment criteria? Was clear constructive feedback given with advice on how to meet required standards? Were varied assessment methods used? Were other assessors involved?*
5. *Have the learner's specific needs been met?*
6. *Was the learner encouraged to play an active role in managing and evaluating their own learning?*
7. *Have there been sufficient learning opportunities?*

Most courses will have set procedures that need to be followed when problems are identified that could lead to a learner failing to meet objectives. This will usually involve alerting the learner's tutor, often leading to a three-way meeting between the learner, the practice educator and the tutor. It is important that you make yourself aware of the procedures by reading programme handbooks or consulting tutors directly. In some situations, when things go seriously wrong, it will be necessary for you in consultation with the university and your managers to terminate the placement immediately. The handbook provided by the university and your own organisational policies will set out the grounds for taking such serious action.

Whether a tutor is involved or not, once a problem is clearly identified that could lead to failure it is important to provide the learner with the opportunities and support to work towards achieving their learning and assessment objectives. This normally involves working together to develop an action plan. The action plan should have clearly stated objectives, target times for achievement of objectives and a date set for a review. Learners need to be actively and (hopefully) positively involved in seeking solutions to the difficulties that have arisen (Sharp and Danbury, 1999).

Managing failing or marginal learners can be difficult for everyone. For social work students their placements represent key components of their qualifying education and the cost of failure is very high, with extreme implications for all involved (Parker, 2008). The student will already have invested time and considerable amounts of money in reaching this point in their education and failure or even the possibility of failure can be devastating. The stress of the situation they are facing may make it difficult for them to fully engage in learning tasks and you will need to take their emotional reaction to their situation and its impact on their learning into account – for instance, making sure that feedback is fully understood. They may become angry and resentful and seek to place blame with others. This can sometimes lead to a serious deterioration in the relationship with you, as the practice educator, and other team members. This can be a very stressful situation for you as well as the student and it is important that you ensure that you have good support networks in place and are able to discuss the strategies that you are adopting with your line manager or practice learning co-ordinator.

CASE STUDY 4.4

Beate, the student whom we met in Chapter 2, is now 50 days into her placement. On her second day the manager, Suli, who was also her practice educator, had returned to work and was full of apologies for not being there for Beate's first day. In Beate's view the first few weeks of the placement went well and she was reasonably pleased with her induction. Unfortunately the residential project was not full and Beate had been able to work with only three residents, two of whom were at college all day. She was rather disappointed that there were no other staff – because resident numbers were low, Suli was often the only other person working at the project and she spent most of her time in the office.

The residents liked Beate very much and said she was a lot of fun to be with. Beate felt she was doing OK and enjoyed spending time chatting to people. She did everything that she was asked to do when she was at the project and had been on a few visits to other agencies.

Suli's view was a little different from Beate's. Beate had been late ten times since the beginning of the placement and had not turned up at all on three occasions. Beate always had a 'good' reason, but consistently failed to comply with the manager's request to phone if she was going to be late or not come in. Suli was finding it difficult to know what to do – Beate's practice was generally of a good standard (although the workload was low and she had not really been tested) but her timekeeping and reliability were unacceptable and she would not be able to meet requirements of the PCF. She had talked to Beate in supervision about this issue and was always told that it would not happen again. Beate is generally happy and bright and the relationship with Suli has largely been positive and open.

ACTIVITY 4.2

What do you think is going wrong in this placement and why do you think Beate is falling short of expectations?

What would you include in an action plan to help Beate improve her performance?

Comment

You should be able to identify a range of problems, some of which are within Beate's control and others that are not. The action plan must address all of these problems if it is to have any chance to succeed.

Although dealing with failing placements is difficult, the risk of passing an incompetent or unfit student means that uncomfortable actions do need to be taken when concerns become evident. Furness and Gilligan (2004) advocate early intervention when failure becomes a possibility, with a rigorous evaluation of the placement from all angles, including learning opportunities and suitability of the practice area. They report that some practice educators working with first-placement students have been inclined to give them the benefit of the doubt, particularly if they feel guilty about some aspect of the placement experience. Furness and Gilligan (2004) are clear that this can be damaging both for the student and for service users that the student may work with subsequently, and stress the importance of acting on concerns.

Element 7: Evaluating the learning experience

Every learning experience that you facilitate as a practice educator will be unique. Each learner and course that you work with will provide you with potential for reflection on your experiences and consequential professional growth. In order to evaluate the placement, you will need to gather information from the learner, from colleagues, from service users and from carers. You can bring this information together with your own thoughts and feelings to evaluate the placement as a whole. You will be able to draw out points of learning for you, for the learner and for your organisation. It is a good idea to undertake some or all of this evaluation with the learner – continuing the learning partnership and bringing it to a logical conclusion. In Part Four we will develop this theme further and look at how you can learn from your experiences and continue to develop as a practice educator.

However, it is important not only that you continue to develop your skills as a practice educator but also that the organisation that you work in continues to develop and become a more effective environment for learning. Peter Senge introduced the concept of learning organisations in the early 1990s. A learning organisation is one that engages with systematic thinking, team working and work-based learning of all forms. A learning organisation will be an effective organisation because the learning of individuals is integrated into the whole. Learning organisations should avoid the same mistakes being repeated and provide an environment in which workers can respond flexibly to new challenges (Senge, 1990; Gould, 2000).

Within a learning organisation each worker has a responsibility for their own personal commitment to continuous development as well as a shared responsibility for supporting the development of others. Within such an environment it is clearly important to learn from experiences of supporting learning in the workplace. To do this, each learning experience should be evaluated and the results of this evaluation incorporated into planning future learning opportunities.

Shaw (2004) suggests that for evaluation to make a real contribution to the development of an organisation there must be:

- an evaluation culture which sustains honest enquiry;
- a commitment within the organisation to development (in other words, the results of the evaluation will be taken on board by the organisation, not just the practice educator);

- learning-based practice (the evaluation must lead to changes in practice when necessary).

In this respect an organisation must have structures that enable the dissemination of information across levels and be able to develop and redevelop meaning for itself to bring about change (Wenger, 2000; Nixon and Murr, 2006).

If you are working as a practice educator for a social work student you will not only need to be involved in evaluating your experience within your own organisation but will also be required to complete an evaluation for the university so that they can monitor the quality of the placements that their student has undertaken. The student will also complete an evaluation. Universities placing social work students will have their own systems for evaluating placements and you will need to contribute to these for each placement that you are involved in. There are currently plans to introduce a standardised national system for evaluating placements: the Quality Assurance for Practice Learning framework (QAPL).

ACTIVITY 4.3

How will you go about evaluating learning opportunities that you support as a practice educator?

Are there mechanisms in place to ensure that your own learning and that of your learner can contribute to your organisation's learning and improve support and opportunities or future learners?

How will you ensure that what you learn from the evaluation will help inform others in your organisation?

Comment

There is a danger that evaluation can become a superficial process – a tick-box exercise. Think carefully about the evaluation and communication systems that are currently in use in your organisation and consider whether they really do help both you and your organisation to learn from your experiences.

Summary of Part One Domain A

- The central importance of the effective management of the learning experience to ensure that:
  - the needs of the learner are met;
  - the learner can balance their learning with their workload;
  - all other people within the work environment are both considered and respected and are not significantly disadvantaged as a result of the learning taking place.

- The importance of developing a learning partnership, which encourages the learner to take an active role in the management of their own, learning – increasing the likelihood that learners will be supported with the development of their professional capability.

- The way that learning is co-ordinated, and therefore that the practice educator's role in this process, will vary significantly depending on the nature of the learning that is taking place and on the specific needs of each individual learner.

- In addition to the direct support of learning in the workplace, that practice educators can also play a role in ensuring that individual and group learning feeds into broader organisational learning.

- Key elements in the effective organisation of work-based learning:
- effective planning and preparations;
- setting clear expectations;
- providing an effective learning environment;
- ensuring effective communication;
- providing appropriate support and monitoring progress;
- undertaking regular reviews;
- evaluating the learning experience.

FURTHER READING

Beverley, A and Worsley, A (2007) *Learning and teaching in social work practice.* Basingstoke: Palgrave Macmillan.
A very readable guide to learning and teaching in social work, covering the necessary learning theory as well as the key aspects of the learning partnership.

Maclean, S and Lloyd, I (2008) *Developing quality practice learning in social work.* Rugeley: Kirwin Maclean Associates Ltd.
Section B A very readable practical guide for practice educators.

Neary, M (2000) *Teaching, assessing and evaluation for clinical competence.* Cheltenham: Nelson Thornes.
Although this book is written for nurses, much of the material covered can be applied to social work learning. Chapter 2 is particularly useful.

Parker, J (2006) Developing perceptions of competence during practice learning. *British Journal of Social Work*, 36 (6), 1017–36.
Useful research on how people perceive their learning.

Part Two
Domain B: Enable learning and professional development in practice

The material in this part links to the following domain standards.

Domain B: Enable learning and professional development in practice

1. Teach the student using contemporary social work models, methods and theories relevant to the work, powers and duties, and policy and procedures of the agency, demonstrating the ability for critical reflection.

2. Establish the basis of an effective working relationship by identifying learners' expectations, the outcomes which they have to meet in order to demonstrate competence, and their readiness for assessment. Agree the available learning opportunities including multi-professional contexts, methods, resources, and timescales to enable them to succeed.

3. Discuss, identify, plan to address and review the particular needs and capabilities of learners, and the support available to them. Identify any matters which may impact on their ability to manage their own learning.

4. Discuss and take into account individuals' learning styles, learning needs, prior learning achievements, knowledge and skills. Devise and deliver an appropriate, cost-effective teaching programme, which promotes their ability to learn and succeed.

5. Make professional educational judgements about meeting learners' needs within the available resources, ensuring the required learning outcomes can be demonstrated in accordance with adult learning models.

6. Identify which aspects of the management of the learning and assessment programme learners are responsible for in order to achieve their objectives. Describe and agree the roles of the work-based assessor in mentoring, coaching, modelling, teaching and supervision.

7. Establish how the learning and assessment programme is to be reviewed. Encourage learners to express their views, identify and agree any changes and how disagreements on any aspects of it are resolved.

8. Advise learners how to develop their ability to manage their learning. Deal with any difficulties encountered by them.

9. Support the student in gathering evidence according to programme requirements.

Additional learning outcome for practice educators at Stage 2

1. Apply an appropriate range of supervisory models, roles and skills, which recognise the power dynamics between assessor and learner.

Introduction to Domain B

So far we have seen that your role as an educator is to enable the development of competence and capability, i.e. to develop people who will be effective career-long practitioners, able to work independently, deal with complexity and embrace change. In addition, we have established the overall ideals of working in partnership with the learner and of promoting self-direction within the learning environment.

Part One has shown that getting to know a learner is a key part of developing the ideal partnership, and, in order to optimise practice learning and assessment, learners' needs and expectations need to be met through a well-structured and organised learning experience. Part Two takes the next step and looks at how to provide suitable learning opportunities that also incorporate the ideals of partnership and self-direction, and which enable the type of learning and professional development that generates competence and capability.

Part Two's chapters relate to four key aspects of enabling learning and professional development in practice.

Chapter 5. Understanding learners.
Chapter 6. Developing learning objectives.
Chapter 7. Considering learning theories.
Chapter 8. Designing learning opportunities.

Before we start, we need to understand that the goal of developing competent and capable practitioners (whether they are students, novices or experienced workers) influences each of these four aspects of enabling learning and professional development in practice. It does this by setting certain standards or underpinning requirements from the outset.

For understanding learners (Chapter 5), our goal demands that learning is about developing learners' critical thinking and practice, and this involves enabling the development of their own personal approach and understanding of practice. Understanding learners is therefore underpinned by a requirement to enable learners to take an active part in their learning and for them to adopt as independent an approach as possible within the boundaries of safe and acceptable social work practice.

However, it can be seen that one of the main dangers here is assuming someone is ready to be enabled in this way. If a learner is not used to taking an active role in their own learning, or to thinking independently with the material or ideas they are provided with, it can be a source of great anxiety. For example, a mature practitioner who has known only a more traditional style of education will probably need a great deal of support before they are able to learn more independently. However, another mature student may be quite confident and fairly self-directive from the start because they have previously undertaken a distance learning course.

Understanding learners, therefore, requires you to be able to adopt a critical and flexible style that seeks out and allows for individual difference when enabling learning. This is where you can embed your learner-centred approach further by truly understanding learners and being able to work from where they are, rather than where you assume them to be, or would prefer them to be.

> ### REFLECTION POINT
>
> *Social work values suggest that each person has to be seen and valued as an individual. A learner-centred approach to enabling learning inherently adopts such a position because it respects and adapts to the learner's perspective (Prosser and Trigwell, 1999). Think about your anti-oppressive approach to people as a social work practitioner and how this can be transferred into your role as a practice educator.*

For developing learning objectives (Chapter 6), our overall goal of developing competent and capable practitioners demands a holistic view of practice learning and social work tasks. As we have seen, social work practice involves more than just a thorough understanding of explicit regulatory competences. In a learning context, placing too much emphasis on competence-based learning and assessment has a number of inherent dangers, because focusing on definable skills and outputs alone can limit and reduce what practice is about (Doel, et al., 2002). There is also a need to be aware of the more implicit processes that guide and inform our decisions and actions, such as the use of intuition, deliberation, judgement-making, critical analysis and evaluation, and incorporate them into learning schemes where possible.

When considering learning theories (Chapter 7), our overall goal of developing competent and capable practitioners takes account of the notion that there is no one overall definition of 'learning'. Learning is a very complex and situated phenomenon; different people learn in different ways and the same person will learn differently in different situations. It follows that there is no single 'right' theory or method to enable it. This is a perfectly acceptable and even liberating position to be in. It means a range of theories can be considered critically and used to devise the most appropriate activities which allow learners to develop their personal understanding and approach.

Finally, designing learning opportunities (Chapter 8) will need to enable learners' capabilities for working independently, dealing with complexity and embracing change. These opportunities should aim to maximise the potential for learners to explore, analyse and apply their knowledge in a variety of contexts. This is about enabling learners to develop their individual approach to critical practice, and in turn means that a very creative, active approach is adopted, whether your enabling role is that of a teacher, supervisor, mentor or coach. Learners will need to be exposed right from the start to the idea that there is no one way to practise if they are to be effective career-long practitioners, able to work independently, and deal with complexity and change in a positive way.

As you can appreciate, providing suitable learning opportunities that incorporate the ideals of partnership and self-direction, and which enable the type of learning and professional development that generates competence and capability, is not a goal that is achieved by being given a complete checklist of learning theories, set teaching methods or learning activities. Instead, this part of the book offers a range of ideas that will enable you to understand your learners' learning, consider how to present learners with diverse ways of thinking and acting, and allow a critical review of these learning processes.

Chapter 5
Understanding learners

The first stage in enabling the learning of others is to understand their needs, requirements and behaviour.

Taking a critical approach

Obviously, learners will have prior learning experiences that influence their expectations and assumptions, and getting to know them is a key part of planning and organising learning. However, you will also have previous learning experiences that have influenced your expectations and assumptions. You may unconsciously adopt a particular teaching style because it is the only one you have been exposed to, or believe that learning happens in a certain way because that is the only way you have learnt. Therefore, either party may bring incorrect assumptions or expectations to the new learning experience.

Let's start with you. Before you begin to enable others, it is a good idea to understand more about yourself as a learner and ensure you have already developed yourself to be the type of learner who is independent and self-directing. If you have not done this, it will be relatively difficult for you to enable anyone else to take this type of approach. It is clear that no learning occurs in a vacuum. As an adult learner you bring a wide range of prior learning and experience to this new learning situation. Your previous experience, as well as your beliefs and values, will play a major part in how you view learning and how you 'naturally' teach or enable others. You should have reflected on and explored previous learning experiences to be fully aware of your beliefs, values and style concerning learning, teaching and enabling learning. This will help you define your role as an educator as well your role as a learner for your own studies, and should be an ongoing process. Chapter 12 provides further advice and guidance on this reflective progression for continuing learning and development.

Let's move on to the learner. The process of getting to know the learner may well have started within the planning stages of a placement or in early contact meetings. However, understanding the learner and valuing their perspective is an ongoing and inherent feature of enabling learning rather than a one-off event. As the learning experience gets under way, learners' behaviours, styles and approaches to learning will become more evident, and you need to be aware of this. Another key point is that part of your role is to enable the learner to know themselves, but not all learners will have enough insight, self-awareness or life experience to do this effectively. For example, a second-year qualifying student may be used to a school or university style of learning environment and know how to learn only from lectures and seminars. It is important to allow time throughout the learning experience, for example as a planned supervision item, for reflection and to encourage learners to have a greater awareness of their own limitations and their particular barriers and motivations for learning via activities and/or discussion. By adopting a critical, open and flexible attitude, items such as learning contracts and planned learning schemes can be revisited to take account of emerging needs or changes where necessary.

Having seen the importance of not only understanding and developing the learner but also yourself, as well as the necessary ongoing nature of this task, we can look more closely at the areas you will need to consider.

What do you need to know about learners?

Some of the key factors that can affect a learning experience are:

- motivation;
- anxiety;
- views of knowledge and learning;
- approaches to learning;
- learning styles;
- awareness of competency.

We will look at each of these in turn to see how to develop a more complete understanding of people as learners.

How motivated is the learner?

Motivation is the compulsion that keeps a person within the learning situation and encourages them to learn (Rogers, 2002). Adult learners are assumed to be 'internally' motivated, by factors such as one's own hopes, desires and needs (Knowles, 1990). However, work-based learners are more likely to be externally motivated, by factors such as incentives, rewards and professional requirements. Internal factors have been argued to be the stronger and more enduring force, but external ones can become internalised (e.g. ambitions for promotion leading to personal development), and it is perhaps inappropriate to distinguish the two as entirely separate. For instance, we know of practitioners who express personal fulfilment from undertaking post-qualifying programmes.

You can use an adult learning approach here. As adults are usually more motivated to learn about things that interest them or have relevance to what they want to do (Knowles, 1990), motivating elements can be enhanced by making the learning environment as relevant and as useful as possible for the individual. Key factors appear to be how immediate, attainable and relevant the learning goals are. By taking a learner perspective and working in partnership with your learner, you will be discussing and agreeing upon a learning scheme together, producing goals that are meaningful and which can become the learner's 'own', i.e. internalised.

Working with more than one learner, for example when leading a multi-disciplinary team workshop, can obviously make this more difficult to achieve, but any group of learners will probably have been brought together for a reason or with a particular aim. If you leave enough time in a group session to find out about more individual motivations, and make sure they are addressed in some way, it will reflect a more learner-centred approach.

The 'feel good' factor associated with motivation should continually be reinforced but it is also important to be aware of the demotivating factors in any learning situation, some of which may be beyond our control, such as lack of time for studying, unsupportive colleagues, unhelpful administrative procedures. Those that are under our control, however, need to be kept under constant review.

5.1

e factors which are likely to motivate or demotivate learners during their learning.

Comment

The range of factors should relate to the variables associated with a learning environment (Knowles, 1990): physical (e.g. desk space or other resources), cultural (e.g. team dynamics), psychological (e.g. learner's anxieties) and social (e.g. the relationship between you).

How anxious is your learner?

Anxiety is a key factor in learning. There are a number of reasons why learners may feel anxious.

- They are in a situation where they are not competent.

- They are aware of their 'not knowing'.

- Becoming reflective practitioners means taking extra responsibility for what and how they learn rather than relying on knowledge from an expert.

- Their past and present personal and educational experiences may have a negative impact, making them feel fearful, vulnerable or intimidated in a practice learning environment.

- Social work itself is anxiety-provoking.

- There is the pressure to 'pass'.

Adapted from Horwath (1999)

A person may be confident and self-directing in their university, personal or work life but feel much less confident in a new learning situation. The point is that most people, when out of their comfort zone will feel anxious and this can impair their ability to learn effectively. Anxiety for novice workers tends to make them over-rely on procedures and rules to avoid making mistakes. Anxiety for more experienced workers is apparent when they enter new posts or when their organisation undergoes significant change and they are expected to let go of established ideas and methods. In this type of situation people who are used to being confident and competent in their work suddenly find themselves unsure and less knowledgeable, and as a result they may become destabilised and disoriented learners (Horwath, 1999).

The loss of competence and of morale therefore combine to make any learning difficult. If someone in a learning situation is feeling unsure and/or unsafe, they may:

- become defensive or angry;
- become 'needy';
- withdraw;
- start to demand the 'right' answers;
- try too hard to please.

The point is that a person in any of these modes of behaviour will not want to, or be able to, learn effectively, and so it is your responsibility to ensure not only that anxiety-making factors are lessened, but that any signs of anxiety like these are noted early on and the root cause uncovered.

How does your learner view knowledge and learning?

One important underpinning factor associated with a person's view of learning is their view of knowledge (i.e. the material being learnt: ideas, theories, methods, etc.). People have different ways of viewing knowledge, ranging from believing that things are either right or wrong, to building up valid knowledge for a particular situation but remaining open to other views (Hofer, 2002). For example, we may know people who believe that their choice in music is the right one and who scorn alternative views; whereas other people who like one particular style of music also expect others to have different tastes and actively listen to alternative styles of music to widen their appreciation.

RESEARCH SUMMARY 5.1

Baxter Magolda (1996) undertook a study of American students, interviewing them about their beliefs and ideas about knowledge and knowing throughout their college and early career years. She noted how their ideas developed over time and developed this range of beliefs into four stages of 'knowing'.

1. Absolute
People at this stage think there are 'right' answers out there to be found, and knowledge is seen as certain or absolute. They become especially anxious with uncertainty and will be looking for anything that can be applied to solve it.

2. Transitional
People at this stage have doubts over the certainty of knowledge. They can see that there are many answers but they still rely on others to tell them which is the right one for a situation.

3. Independent
People at this stage have begun to have an opinion of their own and think through issues and express themselves, but there is little judgement of knowledge, opinions and beliefs, so all views (informed and uninformed, relevant and irrelevant) may be considered equal and unchallengeable.

4. Contextual
At this stage a person's knowledge is constructed for particular situations, considering the relevant conditions and using appropriate evidence. Their understanding is therefore based on evidenced propositions or reasons for that context but can still be challenged as the person remains open to other ideas and the changing context.

The last stage, looking at knowledge contextually, critically constructing valid meaning for oneself and being able to develop a confident 'knowing' for different situations, aligns well with the critical, questioning and open stance needed for professional capability. This is the level to which we aspire and to which we are enabling others to develop. Therefore, understanding how learners view knowledge is an important factor for enabling learning in a work-based environment. A learner may be viewing knowledge in an absolute way because they are young and inexperienced, or because this is the way they were taught and have continued to think, or because they have become anxious. As seen earlier, being in a new or uncertain situation can affect a person's usual capabilities. Many learners are confident practitioners who usually hold a contextual view of knowledge, but anxiety makes them default to thinking that they need the one 'right' answer and the 'teacher' can give this to them.

ACTIVITY 5.2

How could understanding more about the stages of 'knowing' help you as a enabler of learning to work more effectively with your learners?

Can you suggest any ways that you could work with learners which would be more likely to help them to make the transition to a more advanced stage of knowing – for example, how would you enable a learner to move from absolute to transitional thinking?

Comment

Such understanding allows you to more fully appreciate the learner's perspective and the particular barriers that may be preventing development. You may have thought about some specifically designed activities which allow a learner to see a number of alternative but equally valid approaches to practice. Creating a safe environment that encourages and allows a range of answers and approaches to tasks will also be important.

As we have seen, if learners are at an absolute stage and believe that there is only one right way of doing something (e.g. interviewing a service user), they will be desperate for an expert to show them this one way. If an educator does this there is a particular danger that the learner will not learn to think practice problems through for themselves or try different methods. They may continue to practise with the one way that was shown to them and become entrenched in it. They may always be uneasy with new situations and feel anxious in them, and either become unaware of problems or look to others for solutions to them. They will find it difficult to develop their practice in the future as they will not have understood the fundamental issue about practice knowledge – that it is 'constructed' and 'reconstructed' in an ongoing, critical and developmental way, not 'given' as a complete, ongoing 'truth' from someone else.

Of course, many learners will need direction and support to scaffold their learning in order to achieve this more sophisticated level of thinking and we will explore how best to do this in Chapter 8. The point is that if you provide people with just answers, they may well come to believe that answers are 'out there', and rely on someone else for them. This is what 'learning' then becomes for them – someone telling them something, rather than them working a problem through for themselves with the help of others.

REFLECTION POINT

There is another side to this coin. Think about how you view and talk about types of knowledge (either practical or theoretical). If you discuss practice knowledge as 'right/wrong' ways to do things, it could give a learner the idea that your way is the only way to do it. If you discuss only one theory or model of practice (e.g. a task-centred approach), a learner may think this is the only one they need to consider. Think about the ways you could model a more contextual way of viewing knowledge, and help your learner move towards adopting this view as well and appreciate the complexity of social work practice and theory.

It is therefore important to understand these influencing factors concerning the way people view knowledge and to be very aware of how learners might exhibit them through their behaviour; for example, the type of questions they are asking or the way they discuss a point with you. To help understand this further and see how we might consider a learner's language and behaviour in this way, we can use Säljö's (1979) work, which classified learning into five levels or categories.

1. Learning as an increase in knowledge, acquiring information.
2. Learning as memorising or storing information that can be reproduced.
3. Learning as acquiring facts, skills and methods that can be retained and used as necessary.
4. Learning as making sense or abstracting meaning. Learning involves relating parts of the subject matter to each other and to the real world.
5. Learning as interpreting and understanding reality in a different way. Learning involves comprehending the world by reinterpreting knowledge.

By listening to learners as they talk about the knowledge, skills or values they are learning, it is possible to become aware of the level at which they are viewing them. For instance, I could say that I can still recall my times tables from rote learning them, or I may say that I did geography at school by acquiring the facts about different countries, or I revised for exams by noting all the key details down about a topic, memorising them and reproducing them. The language I am using in the previous sentence is very different from the language I use to describe my learning now. For instance, I would say I am applying and interpreting a range of ideas and values on the job and understanding and evaluating how well they achieve my objectives. Each type of language is associated with very different ways of viewing knowledge and with different levels of learning.

Each of Säljö's (1979) levels will be suitable in different circumstances but, as we can see, levels 4–5 are the more appropriate for developing critical practice and align with a contextual view of knowing and knowledge.

Which approach does your learner take to learning?

Looking at how learners not only view their learning and the knowledge they are dealing with but also at how they approach learning tasks and activities allows us to understand why the same task can be undertaken differently by different learners. Approaches to learning link closely with the levels of learning seen above; they are not personal attributes and it is important to realise that learners are able to adopt or choose any approach. There are two main approaches taken (Marton and Säljö, 1976): surface and deep.

- The surface approach focuses on the acquisition and memorising of information, and on facts and concepts in isolation. Learners cannot distinguish more general principles from examples, and they tend to be unreflective. Learning is largely driven by external motivators such as assessment or employer demands. In social work, these principles align with a limited view of the way people might learn professional competences for assessment purposes, i.e. the tick-box notion. As you will have realised, this matches Säljö's (1979) levels of learning 1–3 above.

- The deep approach matches Säljö's (1979) levels 4–5, i.e. meaning, understanding and application of knowledge; relates previous knowledge; connects to other knowledge; relates and distinguishes evidence and argument; and can relate practice to theory.

Learners tend to be self-motivated and reflective. In social work these principles align with a more developed notion of learning professional competencies where a more cohesive and integrated view allows for professional capability to be developed as well.

Entwistle and Ramsden's (1983) work on students' approaches to studying found a third (strategic) approach.

- The strategic approach: the motivation here is to get the best marks or rewards. The exercise of learning is construed as a game, so that acquisition of technique improves performance and involves adopting well-organised and efficient study methods. The learner focuses on assessment criteria and the teacher's preferences. Here we see where a learner might 'get away' with a tick-box approach if the assessment methods take account of only the more mechanistic processes, rather than allowing for the transferable skills necessary for capability as well. However, if the learner perceives that the teacher and/or assessment criteria require something more deep and critical, then learning can be driven in this direction.

As a deep approach is more able to take account of uncertain and complex situations, learning and assessment opportunities should be designed explicitly to align with this approach (Biggs, 2003). These ideas will be developed further in the following chapters within this part of the book. However, the approach learners choose or adopt will be related to their perception of learning, perception of the task, motivation and previous experience.

Individual learners will view learning activities differently and will approach them in different ways. For example, you may have arranged for two qualifying students to shadow you in order to appreciate the complexity of a case review meeting and discuss it afterwards. One student may just watch the proceedings, the other may think about what is happening as they watch and therefore be much better prepared for the discussion. It is what the learner does that counts in the end (Biggs, 2003). The point is that you need to be explicit about what you are expecting from learners but also understand the ways they are interpreting this, rather than make assumptions; otherwise their approach may not be what you intended. To enable a deep approach to be adopted whenever possible, you will need to understand what is happening from the learner's perspective, be able to work from this starting point, and help the learner develop where necessary.

ACTIVITY *5.3*

What would encourage you to learn in a deep or surface way?
What state of mind would a learner need to be in to adopt a deep learning approach?

Comment

Deep learning can be encouraged by the right style of learning and assessment opportunities, i.e. the ones which align more with Säljö's higher levels of learning. Of course, it can also be dependent on having the necessary respect, safety and space to engage in critical thinking and open discussion. In contrast, learning environments in which an educator only tells the learner about things and imposes their own thoughts and ideas, will encourage surface learning. With regard to a learner's state of mind, the bottom line is that the learner is responsible for their own learning. Having a firm partnership based on mutual respect, being motivated and feeling safe are therefore key underpinning factors which may allow a learner to not only appreciate the level of learning required, but want to engage in it.

Which is the learner's preferred learning style?

Most learners will also have preferences for learning in a certain way, i.e. using certain methods or strategies. This learning style will be the way they learn most naturally as individuals, either through habit or preference. There are many different styles. Honey and Mumford's (1982) model, based on Kolb's (1984) experiential learning model, identifies four main learning styles.

- Activist
  - Enthusiastic for new experiences and may rush into them.
  - Can get hooked on what is happening in front of them.
  - May get bored by having to stop and consolidate ideas.
  - Can centre everything on themselves – even group discussion.

- Reflector
  - Observes and evaluates experiences from several different perspectives.
  - Collects data and considers evidence before deciding on action.
  - May be overly cautious and distant.
  - Likes to fully understand a discussion before making their point.
  - May seem distant but tolerant.

- Pragmatist
  - Enjoys experimentation and practical application of ideas and theories.
  - Can get frustrated by open-ended discussion.
  - Prefers active problem-solving.
  - Sees opportunities as a challenge.
  - May also rush into action.
  - Tends to look for better or more practical ways of doing things.

- Theorist
  - Will usually think problems through logically and systematically.
  - Can be a perfectionist.
  - Likes to analyse.
  - May not be able to think laterally.
  - Can prefer certainty to subjective judgement.
  - May be detached and analytical.

This is one of the best recognised models, but there are other types of learning styles that have been identified, such as those associated with the notion of 'multiple intelligences' (Gardner, 1993), i.e. intelligence involving auditory, visual and kinaesthetic (body movement) skills and abilities. There is, however, considerable debate surrounding the reliability of learning styles and their use (Smith, 2001; Coffield, et al., 2004), but they may still have a place in helping both learners and educators understand more about their methods and preferences.

It is important to realise that no one learning style is better than any other; all have strengths and weaknesses. Some people have a strong preference for one particular style, while others are more balanced. Knowing a learner's preferred style can be useful because it can indicate how a learner may learn most effectively. A good match between the style of a learning activity and a learner's preferred style should maximise learning potential, but if there is a mismatch between the two, learning may be hindered.

However, learners need help to learn different skills and abilities (and therefore learning styles) in order to achieve certain outcomes. The question of whether you match a learner's preferred style with a learning activity or alternatively design the activity to stretch the learner to become more versatile would need to be judged for each individual and situation. For example, if a qualifying student, Nadir, is more naturally 'activist' but you require him to critically reflect on case notes and apply and justify social work methods and models with you in supervision before he acts, he may need extra support to see the importance of this and to find a process of reflection and application that works for him. It may be relatively easy to think of singular active or more reflective activities for a student to engage in, but to try to make an active task more reflective and a reflective task more active may be more challenging.

Another issue is that we all tend to teach as well as learn in our preferred style and this may not be appropriate for an individual learner, or all learners within a group. Your preferences for learning in a certain way will affect your assumptions about others too. For example, you might assume that Nadir would want to think and reflect on case notes first before meeting a service user, but as he has a preferred activist style it may seem like wasting time to him. As noted earlier, if you are enabling the learning of another you should have reflected on and explored your previous learning experiences in order to be fully aware of your beliefs and values concerning learning and teaching, and this should include knowledge of your preferred learning style. This point also reinforces the need to continually work towards understanding learners and their perspective, work in partnership with them and allow their input into the learning experience.

CASE STUDY 5.1

Tom met the newly qualified social worker he was mentoring, Yasmin. She was a mature, confident practitioner, having been a care worker with children before qualifying, and also had dyslexia. Tom gave consideration to Yasmin's learning style and they looked at how Yasmin learnt in practice. Yasmin told Tom she learnt best from observing, doing and then reflecting on what had happened. Therefore, in order to promote Yasmin's learning, Tom decided she would observe him in practice preparing and carrying out a reassessment with a service user who was recovering from a stroke, as this was a piece of work Yasmin was to carry out. Afterwards, they used a supervision session to reflect on the intervention that had occurred, what had gone well or not and what had been learnt. In this discussion Tom could see that although Yasmin was an effective practitioner she was not asking the right level of questions which would have shown a more developed understanding of the service user's condition and needs. A lack of specialist knowledge was preventing her from appreciating the service user's capabilities.

Tom knew Yasmin would also need to undertake some independent reading/study into the subject of strokes to give her a wider breadth of understanding. However, Yasmin said she found textbooks and journals difficult to read. Tom encouraged her to gain the necessary knowledge in ways she found more appropriate. She contacted the hospital social work team to see if she could shadow a ward round/meeting on the stroke ward to gain a greater understanding of the effects of strokes. She also contacted the Stroke Association for literature and information and also looked at the internal training manual for relevant courses.

By allowing Yasmin the flexibility and freedom to self-direct her learning at this point, Tom ensured that the most effective learning took place.

Is the learner conscious of their competency or incompetency?

The 'conscious competence model' (unattributed, cited in Atherton, 2009b, and Chapman, c.2009) shows four stages associated with learning new skills. The stage at which a learner may be within this model may be another factor that affects their learning ability.

Stage 1: Unconscious incompetence

This is the 'ignorance is bliss' state where we do not know what we do not know. Making learners aware of their ignorance will probably create anxiety, but it is an important stage in developing motivation. For example, you may have been unaware of the 'stages of knowing' or 'stages of learning' theories looked at earlier in this chapter but hopefully this hasn't made you feel too anxious, as they are being introduced to help you to understand the issues at hand, not to make you feel inadequate. However, if your learner has a vested interest in not doing certain things or in doing things only in their established way, this will also involve another stage of 'unlearning', which will need to be fully supported in partnership.

Stage 2: Conscious incompetence

We are aware of what we don't know. This should engender greater motivation towards finding out more, but only if what needs to be learnt is seen as relevant and useful. We also hope that you will be motivated to find out more about the stages of knowing and other theories in this book and to start applying them as you can see their significance and usefulness for yourselves.

Stage 3: Conscious competence

We are aware of what we do know. In many circumstances after learning has taken place this stage may be perfectly adequate, at least for a time. For some skills, especially advanced ones, we can regress to previous stages if we fail to practise and exercise them. How many of us have learnt to do something on a computer and then completely forgotten how to do it a couple of weeks later if we did not have the chance to redo it.

Stage 4: Unconscious competence

We can use our knowledge without thinking about it. For example, this easily applies to basic skills such as driving or swimming, i.e. the kind of thing we can do without thinking. However, this can also refer to a situation where we know something but do not know how we know it and probably cannot express it (e.g. our more intuitive understandings and hunches). If we are asked about a good piece of practice our answer will fail to do justice to the complexity of what we have done. By encouraging at least some articulation of it, an educator will enable learners to claim credit for what they know and can do, making it meaningful and relevant.

Remember, practice educators commonly assume learners are at stage 2 and aware of the existence, nature and benefit of any new skill (just like they are), and therefore aim towards achieving stage 3. In fact learners may be only at stage 1 and have none of this awareness. The challenge for you is to make them aware in a learner-centred and supportive way. They may think they know all they need to know and, of course, this means you will also need to address their motivation too. Not doing this can be an underlying reason for the lack of success of a lot of training and teaching, especially for more mature or experienced practitioners.

N POINT

re is another side to the coin here. If you are at stage 4 in certain areas of your ice, how can you teach the things you are unconsciously competent at? For example, imagine you are helping a student to develop their practice and you instinctively know how best to encourage an abused child or adult to talk to you. Would you be able to explain to the student the subtle signs you are looking for as well as the techniques you use? Do you ever review these more tacit parts of your practice?

Some authors have suggested the addition of a fifth stage. Baume (2004) says this is a stage of 'reflective competence' where he is:

> ...additionally looking at my unconscious competence from the outside, digging to find and understand the theories and models and beliefs that clearly, based on looking at what I do, now inform what I do and how I do it. These won't be the exact same theories and models and beliefs that I learned consciously and then became unconscious of. They'll include new ones, the ones that comprise my particular expertise. And when I've surfaced them, I can talk about them and test them.

At this fifth level, practitioners are consciously aware of some of the unconscious or subconscious abilities they are using, and are able to analyse, adapt and enhance their activity. They understand why they are doing something and make mindful but subtle changes in light of this understanding. This, of course, aligns with critical thinking, capability and critical practice very neatly. There is an interesting debate and some clever applications of this feature on the www.businessballs.com website.

ACTIVITY 5.4

Make a 'mind map' or 'spidergram' to note down and connect your understanding of the ideas presented to you so far; for exmaple, views of knowledge and learning, approaches to learning and conscious competency. (Search for 'mind maps' on the internet, e.g. using Google, if you are unsure of how to do them.)

Comment

The common features associated with higher levels of knowing and learning, deep learning and reflective competence appear to all relate to our notions of active, independent, reflective and critical thinking.

Chapter 6
Developing learning objectives

Obviously, understanding learners, their views about learning and knowledge, their approaches to learning, and their learning styles, etc., are underpinning factors to enabling learning. However, if we don't have a thorough understanding of what learners will be able to do as a result of their learning as well, and can explicitly state this, then we cannot effectively plan to help them achieve it, or know when they have. This is our next stage in enabling learning.

The 'constructive alignment' approach (Biggs, 2003) allows the design of a learning scheme to begin with the question *What do we want the learner to be able to do as a result of learning?*, and aligns all learning, teaching and assessment strategies to these outcomes in order to optimise the conditions for learning. Such outcomes or learning objectives will at some point be discussed with your learner and this will be where the learner's own goals will be taken into account properly. Again, a critically reflective and flexible approach can be taken to these objectives to ensure you can review and change them where necessary as the learning experience progresses.

General principles

Learning objectives should include:

- content;
- level;
- clear terms;
- support and review points.

Specify the content

It is important to identify the overall content of the learning scheme early on. This may be set to a large extent by other bodies, for example the Professional Capabilities Framework (CSW, 2012). In other circumstances the needs of the team or the organisation may dictate the topic area of a team development session; for example, the specific requirements of a new piece of legislation or policy. By mapping out the areas to be covered it is easier to prioritise, focus and then plan the learning scheme(s). There may indeed be a long list of professional competencies, outcomes or standards to be aware of and 'cover' for learners undertaking a degree in social work or for newly qualified workers, and therefore you may need to collate and prioritise the most relevant areas first.

Once this is done, analysis of the particular area of practice can be undertaken with the three domains of knowing, acting and being, or 'head, hand and heart', so that a holistic view of that area of practice is established at the outset.

- The learner should know about... knowledge (the theory, research, policy, legislation associated with the area of practice).
- The learner should know how to... skills (the related, specific procedures, processes, practice abilities, e.g. clear communication).
- The learner should be aware of... values (anti-discriminatory practice, ethics, etc.).

Setting out these areas early on in the process can ensure the development of practice capability as well as competence right from the start and ensure that important but less measurable aspects such as values are not just added on later.

CASE STUDY *6.1*

Aida worked in a community drop-in centre and was allowing Laura to shadow her as a first-year placement. Aida wanted Laura to see ways to approach and talk to the people using the centre. Later on, after a discussion, Aida was hoping Laura would be able to introduce herself and start to chat to them by herself. Aida's initial attempt at writing a learning objective began with a general statement: 'You will be able to communicate well with people using the centre'. She soon realised that it was ineffective as it did not tell Laura anything about what she needed to do; for example, the type of behaviour, words, or actions that would be acceptable. The objective needed to be broken down further and relate to this situation.

This was not an easy exercise to do. Communication covered such a wide range of skills and abilities; for example, open questioning, eye contact, appropriate contact. How could she put all this in one objective? Aida realised it required a sharp focus on one particular aspect. She decided to use their discussion after the shadowing experience to hear what Laura thought 'good communication' was and the areas she felt less comfortable with, and to concentrate on developing this as a learning objective. One of the things Laura highlighted was the need for firm but sensitive refusal when service users made inappropriate requests, but felt she might be too unassertive to do this. So Aida decided to develop a learning objective with Laura that included understanding more about the nature of assertiveness, its relationship to social work values, and being able to apply this knowledge using appropriate verbal and body-language skills at the centre when necessary. By doing this Aida was able to develop a holistic and meaningful learning objective in partnership with Laura.

Indicate the level of learning

The overall features of any learning can usually be categorised according to a hierarchy like the one seen earlier (Säljö, 1979). For example, the level of learning required to understand a particular section from the direct payments scheme is lower than that required to able to use and critically apply parts of the scheme to deal with the needs of a vulnerable service user. Here we can now use Bloom's (1956) hierarchy to show that learning involves different cognitive (thinking) processes; from simple to more mechanistic levels of remembering, to then being able to break knowledge apart, put it together and subsequently to judge or measure it.

- Recognition and recall – memorise, identify, recognise.
- Comprehension – understand.
- Analysis – break down into parts.

- Synthesis – putting together with other knowledge to form new concepts.
- Evaluation – assess the value of the new knowledge in respect of needs and aim.

The model above is still accepted, but the revised version below adds the important new category of creating knowledge (an extremely relevant addition when we think about professional capability) and moves from using nouns to more active verbs (Anderson and Krathwohl, 2001). These verbs are:

- remembering;
- understanding;
- analysing;
- applying;
- evaluating;
- creating.

It is suggested that the 'higher' levels of learning cannot be addressed effectively until the 'lower' ones have been achieved. For example, if you want learners to use and critically apply direct payments guidance to a particular service user who is disabled, they will first need to have read and understood it. This will need to be built into the learning scheme in ways appropriate to their situation and particular needs. There are also implications here for the way learners perceive learning. As we have seen, a deep learning approach and a contextual way of knowing are both associated with higher cognitive levels: understanding, evaluating and applying knowledge, and constructing individual meaning. However, without first developing underpinning awareness and understanding, or having the ability to analyse, critique and synthesise ideas, your expectations for a deeper approach may not be able to be achieved by the learner.

The best way to approach this issue is by designing the 'lower' levels or more basic stages of learning as part of an overall deeper approach. Reading and understanding can be presented as necessary starting points but in order to align with a deep rather than a surface approach you can ensure they are 'taught' in constructive, critical and active ways. This is an important point that has implications for the way you write the learning objectives, structure the learning tasks, use a learner's prior experience and support learning.

Ensure clarity of terms

Learning objectives need to state what learners will be able to do as a result of their learning and you can use the language of Bloom's (1956) hierarchy to express this. Using the direct payments example mentioned above, the objective might be: To apply the direct payments guidance to a particular case.

As you will be requiring learners to perform their understanding of these outcomes, the criteria used should also be clear, that is, identifying key aspects to show how well you want this to be done. This will also enhance the motivational aspects as detailed above; goals or outcomes need to be explicit, achievable and relevant. Learners therefore need to know what the behaviour or skill 'looks' like in practice so they can compare what they are doing with what is required, identify any gaps and engage in appropriate action to close them. In this way, learners become more empowered and enabled to take control of their learning and work towards greater self-direction.

Also, by knowing how well a learning outcome needs to be achieved, the educator and the learner will be able to tell more accurately if and when the learner is achieving it and have a tool by which to identify any problem areas more directly. This has the benefit of taking the onus off the learner as a 'person' and placing it onto the 'task' instead, making feedback less personal and more useful, an important point we will return to later. This also impacts on other aspects of the learning process, such as assessment and facilitation, as outcomes provide the criteria to judge levels of achievement and to see where learners are going wrong. Learners have a fundamental need to know exactly what they are aiming for in order to know how well they are doing and how to do it better.

In the direct payments example, the level of analysis and type of evaluation required could be stated as follows.

1. Read and analyse the guidance.
2. Identify the aspects that are relevant to the case notes for Mrs X.
3. Generate a number of options for action that can help Mrs X.
4. Evaluate each in respect of social work values.

Include support and review points

Having explicit learning objectives and criteria, being aware of the level of learning expected, and also the knowledge, skills and values involved within the objective, allows you to develop a more detailed structure for learning. This, in turn, allows for fuller understanding of the learning process and for an explicit learning scheme to be developed. The support associated with each stage within the scheme can also be identified and is, of course, judged in respect of the learner's level, particular needs, etc., and their previous experience.

As we have seen, previous knowledge and experience are key components of adult learning and need to be taken account of when planning a learning scheme. This allows for key skills and requirements to be built in as necessary and ensures the scheme is aligned to, and is useful for a learner's needs. For example, in the scheme above the discussion of options for action in stage 4 could highlight similar examples the learner has dealt with in the past.

However, there are a number of dangers to be aware of. First, although prior experience (whether learning, knowing, or doing things) can be of enormous value as a building block or starting point for any learning programme, it can also act as a barrier. A learner will feel safer with material they already know and may be reluctant to question it even though it is incorrect or inappropriate for the new situation. Second, we may mistakenly expect or assume that learners already possess the necessary knowledge, skill or values to learn in a particular environment. If learners are not achieving a learning objective, the problem may lie with an aspect of their previous experience, or the lack of it. There are a number of scenarios.

- They don't have the appropriate knowledge.
  - They may be unable to proceed with a piece of work because of a lack of information to tackle the problem. In our example the case notes may simply not be accessible.
- They don't have the skills to work with knowledge at the appropriate level.
  - They will not be able to deal with the complexity of linking theories to practice if they cannot analyse the situation in order to find some general principles. In our example the learner may not know how to analyse the written information in the documents.

- They don't have the background, the practical skills or understanding of the appropr
  value base to undertake the task.
  - They may understand the theory behind interpersonal communication but have no
    practical experience of actually talking to a service user, or have seen it from a service
    user's perspective. In our example the learner may not understand the personal
    experience behind the case notes and the implications that has for the range of
    options that might be suitable.

The stages in our example can be more fully articulated to show the appropriate type of
support and the review points.

- Supply the learner with the national and local direct payments guidance and direct her
  to the Directgov website.

- Ensure the learner knows how to access the service user's case notes as she uses the
  same software. However, ensure passwords work.

- Let the learner practise analysing the guidance with more basic examples first.

- Review point. The parts most relevant to Mrs X's situation need to be identified. Discuss
  Mrs X's situation in supervision first to ensure it has been understood on a more
  personal level, before the next stage.

- Tell the learner she can generate at least three ideas to help Mrs X using lists or mind
  maps. Tell her she will be expected to explain and critically reflect on them by herself
  before we discuss them together in supervision.

- Final review – in supervision let the learner explain and reflect on each option without
  interruption before discussing them together.

ter 7
Considering learning theories

We can now consider theories about how learning occurs and look briefly at the ways they can inform practice. Even though human beings are always learning and developing in some way, the activities and processes involved are complicated and are still not fully understood. Consequently, there are a number of theories about how learning occurs; they are all valuable, but there is no one overarching theory. Therefore, when designing ways learners may be enabled to achieve their objectives it is important to recognise the limitations of using learning theories and to think more critically about their use and application in practice.

Because none of the learning theories fully explains learning, they will all be deficient in one way or another for your needs and should not be used exclusively or uncritically. The point is that any concept or model will rarely fit a specific process completely, especially one as unclear as learning. However, critically thinking through any aspects of a theory with the needs and requirements of the learner, and with ideas for particular methods, is useful in itself. It will help you notice any mismatched areas, and your own learning becomes a little deeper as you check your understanding. Presented below is a small selection of learning theories that appear to align with our notion of practice-based learning and a few ideas for their use in practice. Further ideas and theories for consideration may be found in Beverley and Worsley (2007) and in Walker, et al. (2008). A range of learning opportunities is considered in Chapter 8.

Constructivist learning

Views associated with deep learning and contextual knowing particularly align with constructivist learning theories (e.g. Bruner, 1960), which state that there are only individual perceptions of reality, meanings and knowledge rather than external, objective realities. Learning is therefore an individual's active construction of new perceptions, an act of self. If you base learning activities on this theory you would be stimulating and assisting the development of the learner's construction of their own awareness and insight.

Ideas for practice

- Let learners unpick and try to resolve case studies by questioning, thinking and testing out their own ideas.

- Encourage acts of active self-search and discovery, rather than input or transfer your ideas to learners.

Humanistic learning

The idea of being learner-centred follows very humanistic principles (e.g. Rogers, 1980) and places learners and their desire to fulfil their potential at the heart of the learning process.

Aspects such as involving learners in as much planning and design of their learning as possible align with humanistic principles. Your role here is to increase the range of experiences so the learner can use them to achieve their own desired changes.

Ideas for practice

- Let learners set their own personal goals alongside their professional ones.
- Allow learners to use but also extend their existing abilities by designing tasks which challenge them in some way.
- Allow learners to develop their own learning contract.

Social and situated learning

The idea of 'learning on the job' through a type of apprenticeship aligns well with social (e.g. Bandura, 1977) and situated learning theories (e.g. Lave and Wenger, 1991). Social learning theories explain that within any social context people can learn from one another, from observation, imitation, and modelling. Situated learning theory argues that learning is usually unintentional rather than deliberate and is embedded within activity, context and culture. Learners become involved in a 'community of practice' which embodies certain beliefs and behaviours to be acquired (Lave and Wenger, 1991). If work-based learners are learning the language, attitudes, values and practices of the workplace (not just knowledge and skills) via contact with yourself and other practitioners, then this may need monitoring. Your position will automatically be that of a mentor or role model to many learners, providing inspiration and models of good practice, but there may also be another part to play in ensuring that a student or novice worker is not picking up inappropriate attitudes or practices from colleagues.

Ideas for practice

- Ensure learners can observe and follow practitioners as they undertake their tasks.
- Monitor the beliefs and attitudes, as well as the practices, a learner is acquiring.
- Encourage learners to take part in all team activity and meetings.
- Develop your coaching and mentoring skills.

Experiential learning

Experiential learning provides a general acceptance that experience and observations form the basis of learning. It can, however, mean different things to different people.

- Learning from current experience – the experience creates a need for further learning.
- Using past experience for learning – challenging the present.
- Learning by doing – actively engaging in the learning context.

Here, we focus more on 'learning by doing' so that encouraging experiential learning means guiding and facilitating the learner through various elements of the experience, ensuring they become part of the overall learning scheme. As we shall see, most experiential learning models contain a reflective element. The aim of reflection is to draw out the 'learning' from these experiential processes by analysing, identifying and linking the significant incidents to ideas and theories that shed light on them (Beatty 2003, cited Parker, 2004, p47), and to inform future action.

Ideas for practice

- Develop simulations or games for learners.
- Let learners become involved in and reflect on 'live' cases.
- Develop problem-based learning activities.
- Act out and reflect on role play scenarios with learners.

Experiential models

Kolb (1984) developed an explicit model around the key characteristics of learning from experience, based on the work of Dewey, Lewin and Piaget, known as the experiential learning model.

In his model, the process of experiential learning is described as a staged, cyclical process involving the four learning modes. The process of learning may be entered at any stage and it perpetuates itself. Concrete experience is followed by reflection on that experience, then by the identification of general ideas or theories describing the experience, then by the planning of the next experience, leading in turn to the next concrete experience. The key point is that all four stages of the cycle should be apparent within a learning scheme in order for it to be an effective process where knowledge is created through the transformation of experience. As the learner needs to move from being an active participant to an observer, to an analyst and then to an experimenter in order for deeper learning to take place, you would plan for each stage to be a specific part of the learning experience. You would also enable the learner to undertake various processes within each of the stages to maximise the learning. These include designing the learning experience in the first place, encouraging use of reflective models and questioning techniques for the reflective phase, encouraging theory to practice links for the analytical phase and then promoting the use of action plans for the next phase.

Kolb's (1984) model is criticised for being a rather 'technical', staged approach (Miettinen, 2000; Coffield, et al., 2004) and does not take into account the more emotional aspects of learning. Race's (2010) model, although less theoretical, does include these aspects and his elements interact with one another like ripples in a pond rather than progressing through a cycle (Figure 7.1). This creates an integrated, interacting 'whole' that constitutes successful learning and is made up of:

- wanting/needing (motivation);
- doing (trying out; action);
- digesting (making sense);
- feedback (outcomes; reactions).

Figure 7.1 Adapted from Race's (2010) 'ripples' model of learning

The ripples of 'wanting' filter out from the centre through the surrounding layers. From the outside, 'feedback' sends ripples back into the model from the various sources that provide it (e.g. instructors, fellow learners, assessment). 'Doing' and 'digesting' intersect with each other and are influenced by 'needing/wanting' and by 'feedback'. By working with this model, any learning opportunity you design will be driven by the learner's motivation so that the 'doing', the opportunities for 'digesting' or reflecting and 'feedback' are all positively engaged with. Here, your role may be slightly different than if you were following Kolb's model as you may be considering the design of the learning task from a much more motivational angle.

ACTIVITY 7.1

Think about how you 'learn by doing' and design a model (e.g. a diagram or picture) that contains the elements you think are most important and shows how they are connected.

Comment

The way you portray the process will be very individual (we have seen everything from pictures of trees to 'snakes and ladders' in our workshops). The most common elements that are used are, of course, 'doing' and 'reflecting' but a range of personal as well as social elements can be included; for example, planning, discussing, team involvement. In order for any experiential learning to be maximised, though, the processes need to be made explicit and reinforced.

CASE STUDY 7.1

Practice educator Kate wanted Joe, a third-year qualifying student, to critically analyse and evaluate his practice more holistically. Joe was a good practitioner in many ways, but he was adopting a paternalistic attitude to the service users (older adults), which, although caring, was in effect denying them a voice. Kate could see that the compliant responses of a particular service user, Albert, had been more to do with submission than actual agreement with the plans being offered for his future.

Kate discussed a number of reflective activities with Joe, who admitted to being a more activist type of learner than a reflector. The idea of keeping a written journal had a completely demotivating effect on him. They tried other reflective activities such as case discussions and critical questioning, but they were ineffective. Joe was still unable to become fully aware of the effect his overprotective stance was having.

Kate decided to take a different approach and set up a 'game', the object of which was to encourage 'Albert' to speak his mind. Kate wrote down on a set of cards some key enabling phrases but also some of the more disabling phrases Joe had used in practice when discussing Albert's future with him. Joe had to actively role-play the part of Albert while Kate, playing the part of his social worker, read out the phrase on each card. Joe, as Albert, had to rank each phrase between 1 and 10 to show how enabled he felt in being able to express a different view from that being offered. Joe soon began to realise that the phrases and language he used were the more disabling ones because he now heard them with different ears.

Kate had realised that following an experiential learning cycle with Joe meant starting with an active experience from the service user's perspective rather than from his own. She could then sensitively help him reflect and learn from this.

ːtive learning

n and reflective learning theories are, of course, very important to practice learning in
n right, as well as being part of an experiential learning process. We consider certain
aspects of reflective learning here, but also develop a number of ideas further in the next
chapter when we consider how reflective practice can be enabled within a range of broader
learning opportunities.

Schön (1983) suggested that learning can emerge from the analysis of practice through the
process of reflection in two ways: reflection-in-action (while doing something) and reflection-
on-action (after doing something). Even though Schön has been criticised for not describing the
process of reflection adequately (Ixer, 1999; Moon, 1999), there is now an increased emphasis
on learning through reflection and an acknowledgement that 'becoming a professional' is
more than the simple acquisition of knowledge and development of skills. For Boud, et al.
(1985, p19) reflection is an activity in which people *recapture their experience, think about it,
mull it over and evaluate it.* They focus on the key aspects of returning to an experience,
attending to or connecting with feelings, evaluating the experience and integrating the new
knowledge. It is a process that involves, among other things, the consideration of 'self' and
one's own experiences of practice (Doel, et al., 2002).

Limitations and issues – a number of questions to consider

- The lack of clarity over what reflection actually is can make it a difficult activity to
  explain and assess.
  - We may indeed be thinking about what we are doing while we are doing it in
    practice, and making or reviewing on-the-spot decisions; for example, when
    undertaking an assessment. This is a very different type of thinking and reviewing
    from that which we do on an event after it's happened, say in supervision – should
    they both be called 'reflection'?
  - Are reflective processes and outcomes distinguishable?

- Not all experiences are open to analysis and reflection; we have all had intuitive,
  perceptive or insightful moments that defy explanation and are difficult to articulate.
  - Is the thinking or deliberating we do in action actually able to be 'recovered' and
    articulated, or is it too tacit?
  - When we reflect on practice, can we really re-create the situation honestly and our
    thoughts exactly as they were, or is the reconstruction necessarily something
    different, and if so, in what ways?

- Not everyone 'reflects' in the same way.
  - Do you reflect better on paper or in your head, with questions or by considering
    ideas?

There are many ways people reflect and, indeed, it is a very individual activity, rather like
learning. There also seems to be a range of different possible outcomes. We would not like
to prescribe any one method over any other, but there are a few principles relating to the
nature of reflection to take note of.

Principles of reflection

- Reflection should be active.
  Ensure that the reflective process leads to learning or active output. Atkins and Murphy

(1994, cited Rolfe, et al., 2001, p24) point out the need for action in order to fully support reflective practice:

For reflection to make a real difference to practice, it is important that the outcome includes a commitment to action. This may not necessarily involve acts which can be observed by others, but it is important that the individual makes a commitment of some kind on the basis of that learning. Action is the final stage of the reflective cycle.

- Reflection should be holistic and meaningful.
  One of the most important aspects of learning through reflection identified by Ruch (2000) is the idea that there is no attempt to split personal experiences from professional and educational experiences; it is holistic in nature. In other words, reflective learning acknowledges and values the fact that when adults learn something new, all kinds of information from other parts of their lives help to shape that learning and place it in the context of what is already known. Reflection is therefore likely to play a large part in making personal and deep meaning for a learner, and encourage the integration of learning across all three required areas for professional capability – a learner's knowing, acting and being.

- Reflection should be developmental.
  Reflection can be seen as a developmental process in a number of ways (Brown and Rutter 2008).
  - The more explicit methods and outputs of practice usually need to be identified before more implicit aspects such as assumptions and intuition can be unearthed and evaluated for their 'fitness for practice'.
  - Learners may need time to recognise and explore their own particular methods of reflecting.
  - These methods may need to be improved in order to become more deep and critical.

- Reflection should be critical.
  There is a need for reflection to be inherently critical. This is not about you or the learners criticising their practice, rather it means that reflection is able to examine and analyse practice in order to objectively evaluate strengths and weaknesses. Being critically reflective means being able to measure, assess and appraise all aspects of practice so that the learning can enhance and change practice for the better in more fundamental ways. Essentially, a deeper critical thinking approach to reflection is needed so that enhanced capability as well as competence is achieved, i.e. it is not just skills or knowledge that are 'reviewed', rather a new view of practice is achieved as the assumptions or 'givens' associated with certain methods or practices are also scrutinised.

REFLECTION POINT

Critical reflection is necessary for all professionals because on a day-to-day level there are some dangers associated with the development of practice expertise and with a more surface approach to reflection. We can all fall under the very real danger of unquestioningly applying standardised responses in complex situations (Thompson, 2000). These are the purely intuitive or routine methods of practice that help us survive large workloads. Think about your own routines and 'rules of thumb' – are you able to identify and evaluate these habitual practices?

As we can see, an alignment with deep learning and capability means that learning through reflection is a very seductive idea for professional learning and development. However, it is not the only way people learn and may not be suited to more mechanistic skills. As stated earlier, there is no one overarching learning theory.

Enabling critical reflection

Critical reflection can also create doubt, uncertainty and sometimes, like any deep learning, negative reactions. When people are encouraged to reflect on their own learning and practice by others they may experience a very real fear that they will be exposed and demonstrate a lack of knowledge or poor practice through the discussion. This fear can become ever more real in situations where they feel that their practice is under particular scrutiny. Enabling critical reflection is therefore a difficult balance between providing a safe and supported but also appropriately challenging learning situation.

The quality of the relationship between a learner and their practice educator can therefore have a very significant impact on the depth of critical reflection and learning that takes place. Each relationship will be unique and will evolve over time (Beverley and Worsley, 2007), but developing a partnership allows trust and respect to build, which in turn helps alleviate the more negative effects of any power imbalance, past experiences or difference.

There are a number of core elements to be aware of when enabling critical reflection, which we can consider with an example of supervising Rebecca, a newly qualified social worker who is displaying elements of oppressive practice towards mental health patients by believing they are all at risk if they return home.

- Be sensitive and non-threatening, and keep the focus off the person and onto relevant issues around the task, knowledge or skills.
  You could ask Rebecca about the process for assessing risk factors associated with a mental health service user returning home in order to show the wide range of aspects that can be considered.

- Ask open but specific questions which encourage a shift in perception.
  You might ask Rebecca how someone with a mental health issue might be thinking about living back in their own home.

- Ask questions which sensitively challenge and test assumptions and preconceptions and check for prejudice.
  Together you could discuss which particular risks are likely to be more prevalent for people who have had a mental health diagnosis and why.

- Use active listening techniques.
  Pay full attention to the speaker, repeat back what they have said in your own words, summarise, check emotions to show that you understand what they have said and their emotions.
  Your might begin to notice Rebecca's underlying anxiety around taking responsibility for such decisions.

- Ask for concrete examples to test assumptions and clarify understanding.
  You could ask Rebecca whether she has actually seen a particular type of behaviour she is worried about and whether there is evidence of it for this client group.

- Encourage self-evaluation but keep it strengths-based.
  You would allow Rebecca to voice her real concerns around her own accountability in this issue and her unease regarding service users' safety.

- Avoid being judgemental or offering solutions.
  You would challenge Rebecca's thinking but not tell her she is wrong or devalue her opinions. You would work with Rebecca's ideas and assist her to broaden them to look at possible alternatives and outcomes that acknowledge the safety aspect but which do not oppress service users.

The role of others in reflective learning

Reflective learning usually needs to have other people involved to make it more purposeful and more critical. There are limits to how much people can learn from experience if they are reflecting on their own (Ellstrom, 2006, cited Boud, et al., 2006).

- Other people can encourage different and more balanced perspectives. Reflecting alone can become self-justifying or self-pitying. Agyris and Schön (1978) talk about the importance of supporting others to confront their own ideas and explore their unconscious assumptions.

- Other people can provide emotional support through facilitator or peer input. As reflection will involve personal elements and professional risk, facilitators and peers should not only provide explicit and jointly agreed expectations and have modelled the process, but should also be sensitive to key signs of anxiety and distress.

- Other people can ensure the necessary space and time for a learner to undertake such activities. Reflecting on casework can allow the time to slow down and think about different alternatives as well as the potential dangers of 'rushing in' to act in certain cases.

Ideas for practice

- Critical incident analysis.
  Critical incident analysis techniques allow reporting on specific situations and events, and will therefore provide appropriate material for reflection. However, in order to align with our key principles, you and your learner should be clear about (and have agreed on) which elements of the reflective process are appropriate for the situation and the expected outcomes.

- Using frameworks or models.
  Most reflective frameworks offer a series of elements or steps to explore practice experience more fully and critically, providing the structure, focus and scaffolding for learning. They should move a learner away from mere description of events and actions (although this is a necessary starting point), through an examination of particular aims, reasons and decisions within those actions and events, to an evaluation of the outcomes, and further to identification of the learning that occurred for practice plus any changes or actions that are needed. Links and connection with theory, research, policy and legislation can be made where appropriate.
  This is an educator's framework for reflection (based on Gibbs 1998, cited Rolfe, et al., 2001, p32):
  Description – *What happened?*

Feelings – *What were you thinking and feeling?*
Evaluation – *What was good and bad about the experience?*
Analysis – *What sense can you make of the situation?*
Conclusion – *Is there anything else you could have done?*
Action plan – *What was learnt? If it arose again, what would you do?*

There are two key points to be made here. First, the most common elements within reflective models such as these, i.e. description, analysis and evaluation, are all necessary for maximising the learning that such reflection can achieve. Second, reflection can encompass a deeper level of criticality within each of these elements as follows (Brown and Rutter, 2008; Brown, et al., 2010).

- Description – more details than the ones that were initially noted need to be identified so that significant but less obvious features are not lost or ignored. Example – after an observation a student might be asked, Did you notice what the siblings were doing while you were watching the child and mother?

- Analysis – deeper questioning about what happened and why it happened needs to show not only inherent assumptions of the person reflecting, but also the 'givens' associated within the reflective situation itself, and any connections or links between aspects of the event. An open view on the experience or situation is also required by seeking other perspectives, and by exploring a wider range of alternative ideas, decisions, interpretations, actions, etc. Example – at a peer supervision meeting or an action learning group a practitioner might ask, *Do we automatically reject the medical model and how does this affect our attitudes to the people who work with it?*

- Evaluation – judgements on processes and outcomes need to go beyond what worked or didn't and what was learnt, to a deeper level of understanding about the importance, quality and appropriateness of the experience for self and others. This is about judging not only whether something was done right but whether it was the right thing to do and also, perhaps, a reconsideration of how it is decided what is 'right' in the first place, i.e. triple-loop learning as described by Argyris and Schön (1974). This level of criticality is unusual as most of us lack the power to challenge the parameters in which we work. However, sometimes we do need to re-examine fundamental areas of practice that we take as a 'given'. Students have a particular knack of asking naive questions which make us stop and rethink things. Example – a first-year student on a shadowing experience may ask, *How have we decided it is right to take children and place them in a care system where they could be at risk of a different kind?*

- Recording reflections.
The aim of reflective writing is to enable learners to identify, evaluate and personalise their learning and possibly develop and employ strategies to improve this learning and apply it to day-to-day practice. Encouraging the recording of reflective output (either written or via alternative media) can help to ensure the descriptive level is as accurate as possible and encourages deeper learning from this material (Moon, 1999). Of course, a traditional form of journal writing will not suit everyone's learning style and so the method for recording should not become an imposition.
The issue of trust is also important here. It is inconsistent with our main principles, and decidedly oppressive, to insist on learners following specific and prescriptive instructions

to 'make' them reflect and to focus only on negative aspects. Rather, you can make the process and the content the outcome of joint decisions focusing on the wider reflective learning aim, and provide appropriate support and guidance. Learners should also have the right to keep any recordings private, with relevant sections being chosen by the learner to share or use to show their processes. Moon (1999, pp199–202) gives some particularly useful exercises for the process of recording and for giving it a focus; for example, writing from different perspectives, SWOT analysis and imaginary dialogues.

ACTIVITY **7.2**

Think about how critical reflection has played a role in your own learning and in developing your practice. Research various models of facilitating reflection and develop your own model which incorporates the features you think are most important.

Comment

Any model needs to ensure safety for the learner as well as challenge, the opportunity to include successful as well as less successful events, and enable a deep and also critical approach to reflective learning.

If the aim of critical reflection is to evaluate our thinking and actions, it plays a key role in developing critical practice. This will be considered in more detail in the following chapter.

Chapter 8
Designing learning opportunities

Once you have understood learners' needs and perspectives, established the learning objectives and considered the principles behind certain types of learning and associated activities, you can start to make decisions about how best to design and manage the learning opportunities. In other words, you are now asking which learning events are most appropriate for learners and their needs, and how they can achieve the level and approach to learning required. Opportunities can include instructional as well as facilitative methods, but they all should align with our ideals of partnership and self-direction and enable competence and capability. We can revisit our ideas about critical practice and a critical approach to enabling learning and ensure an appropriate approach is taken from the outset.

Developing critical practice

Critical practice is a requirement to work with uncertainty, risk, diversity and difference in a way that recognises oppression, and works to empower and promote the needs and rights of colleagues and fellow workers, as well as users and carers (Adams, et al., 2002). Critical practice is therefore not about 'being certain' (the 'certain' thing is not necessarily the 'right' thing). It is about being able to deal with uncertainty using sound, valid and accountable processes and, where appropriate, maintain a position of 'respectful uncertainty', or at least hold onto doubt for longer and seek out other possible versions (Taylor and White, 2006). This requires the development of a practitioner as a 'critical being', i.e. a person who not only reflects critically on knowledge but also develops their powers of critical self-reflection and critical action (Barnett, 1997). In order to achieve this, learners need directed but risk-free opportunities to critically analyse and evaluate practice, explore alternative approaches wherever possible, and develop their own ways to deal effectively with the continuing complexity of practice.

Ideas for practice

The key point is that you can encourage a deeper, more meaningful approach to learning in most situations. There are some basic but very practical methods that help to facilitate this which you could use within a wide range of learning activities.

- Ensure exploration and discussion from the learner's viewpoint.
- Encourage critical and evaluative comments.
- Allow choice in learning.
- Build on personal knowledge and experience.
- Ensure application to the learner's situations.
- Allow the learner to draw out general principles from specific learning so they may be used in other contexts.
- Give and discuss formative feedback.
- Allow time for reflective opportunities.

It comes back to our initial principles of 'constructive alignment' or 'joined-up thinking' and a clear understanding of learners and what is required from them. If there is a continued mismatch between the input from the educator and the learning approach required, the learner is in effect being taught to either fail or underachieve. Knowing that you are aiming for the learner to adopt a deep approach to their learning will guide the design of learning opportunities in an appropriate direction.

Instructional input

In some situations a basic level of knowledge use or learning is required; for example, acquisition and recall of facts or simple procedures, establishing basic knowledge and understanding before more complex tasks can be undertaken. Even if certain knowledge or skills need to be accepted for the most part unconditionally, or presented in a particular or very simple way, the learning opportunities you manage or design can still encourage learners to develop understanding for themselves.

Let's think this through in more detail with an actual learning opportunity in mind. You may be looking at the assessment process with a student, Mike. You will first need to tell him 'what' it is about, describe the form and the process and allow that description to make sense and be understood. You may show Mike what the assessment form looks like and go through the process of filling one in. You may then allow him to see 'how' the assessment is done by letting him observe you undertake an assessment of a service user, and allow him to practise it.

However, these 'stabilising' features of learning need to be achieved within an overall 'deep approach', rather than a surface one. In order to develop a deeper approach to learning, any stabilising features should be part of a more complete package of learning that develops Mike's individual insight and meaning making as well as his awareness of alternatives. You need to be incorporating more than the 'what' or 'how' by looking at the 'why?', 'what else?', 'how else?' and 'so what?' In this example, it may mean also asking Mike how he really feels about the assessment process and its budgetary constraints, or ensuring he is able to see a variety of different methods by shadowing other social workers, or letting him think of alternative ways to ask assessment questions. This can obviously be done when you judge the time is right for Mike, but it will move any discussion and thinking beyond mere reproduction, description or explanation to more critical and evaluative understanding and interpretation.

> ### REFLECTION POINT
>
> *The problem, as we have described earlier, is that many learners may actually prefer to be just told things and given answers. Nevertheless, your role as an educator is about challenging and developing learners' thinking. Think about the abilities and skills you already possess that can help achieve this sensitively.*

The amount of direct input, structure and provision of material you provide for a learner will probably be dictated by the complexity of the information and the level of self-direction and independence the learner is capable of, or needs encouraging in. In general terms, if a learner is very inexperienced and anxious, or the material extremely complex, your input will be as instructive as necessary to provide a solid framework of understanding and confidence. If the learner is self-directing and confident with the topic, or the topic or skill is relatively simple, the educator's input may be more facilitative and guiding as the learner 'instructs' him or herself. Obviously, this is not a simple equation and the way you choose your methods is very much a contextual and relational process, dependent on the situation. The balance you are trying to achieve is in developing competence and as much capability as appropriate for the learner but with minimal risk to the learner, service users and the organisation.

Ideas for practice

When using a more instructional type of input there are some general principles to be aware of (Atherton, 2009a).

- Advance organisers.
  These are simply devices used in the introduction of a topic which enable learners to orient themselves to it so that they can locate where any particular bit of information fits in and how it links with what they already know. These devices may be outlining handouts, statements of objectives or introductory orienting remarks. They give learners confidence that the educator knows where they are going. They also help learners to get a handle on the session and to see when new material is being introduced.

- Scaffolding.
  The educator provides the external structure within which the learner can build their building. This includes engaging learners' interest, demonstrating, progressing from the simple to the complex, organising material, summarising, providing feedback, and so on.

- Models, metaphors and analogies.
  With simple models the starting point is the simplest possible case of something, and then it is elaborated and moved on to those models that are closer to the real world. Using analogies ('something is like something else because...') needs care because they can be so powerful that learners get hooked on them and may not see where an analogy doesn't fit. Using metaphors needs even more care as you are saying that 'one thing is something else' to suggest the similarity, although not literally.

ACTIVITY 8.1

Use the internet or other sources to find a range of other ideas to show you how to present information and instruct others using various methods (e.g. PowerPoint, handouts, whiteboards). Make a list of key tips and ideas.

Comment

Ideas for stimulating interest and enabling understanding; for example, using diagrams, clear headings and points, should be useful in all areas of your work, from meetings to report writing.

Work-based learning activities

There are a number of established work-based learning activities that are more suited to enable the holistic development of practice values, knowledge, skills and abilities. They will obviously be active and learner-focused in their design. As established earlier, learning activities need to encourage learners to critically analyse and evaluate their practice and provide opportunities to explore alternative approaches wherever possible.

In general, active, experiential and reflective methods appear to be most appropriate for adult learners and to be more effective for developing professional capability. They help reinforce learners' understanding that there is usually more than one possible approach to working in a complex situation and can ensure that integration takes place between all three of Barnett and Coate's (2005) domains of knowing, acting and being. Your role as an educator is to find out more about work-based learning activities and critically evaluate them with the information gathered so far in this process, to ensure the ones you choose are aligned with the learner's needs, etc., and then review your own skills for delivering them. Some broad examples are presented below and further ideas and theories for consideration may be found in texts such as Doel and Shardlow (1998), which provides a wide range of engaging ideas and activities.

Shadowing

Shadowing, the practice of accompanying others to see and learn from their practice (Gould, 2000, p588), is a well-used method of promoting such learning on placement. By shadowing and observing an experienced social work practitioner, some implicit abilities and processes become more visible and so the content of practice becomes more open and accessible (Shardlow and Doel, 1996). Observing a number of practitioners in this way will provide much raw material from which a novice practitioner can develop their own approach.

Demonstrating/modelling

Learning by modelling takes the shadowing activity one step further so that, as well as observing an experienced practitioner complete a skill, a student or novice will imitate the practitioner's behaviour at a later time. As such, it is used as a method for learning very complex behaviours and is one of the more holistic ways to ensure readiness for practice (Shardlow and Doel, 1996).

Role-play

Role-play is any activity when you either put yourself into somebody else's shoes or when you stay in your own shoes but put yourself into an imaginary situation. This is an effective method of making more theoretical material come alive and also for developing interpersonal skills in a safe situation. Role-play can also flag up certain features of a situation more clearly than in real life, which can get bogged down in unnecessary detail.

Case-study work

Case studies can range from simple 'stories' illustrating issues in practice, to complex sets of documentation that may require analysis and evaluation. They work well for developing problem-solving skills and abilities.

Simulations

Simulations set up particular scenarios. It does not have to be the external circumstances that are simulated; the simulation can also be created from the decision-making, skill and practice of the practitioner working with these circumstances. This can allow a 'safer' and less anxiety-provoking environment than working with a real-life case but still allows a sense of urgency for decision-making.

Critical incident analysis

These procedures collect direct observations of human behaviour that have critical significance in a particular arena. These observations are kept track of as incidents, which are then used to solve practical problems and develop broad principles. The analysis should pick out the key parts of the event so that the importance of the processes (actions and responses rather than just outcomes) is understood.

Coaching, mentoring and supervision

Broader types of learning opportunities such as coaching, mentoring and supervision are able to provide the appropriate space, freedom and lack of risk which enables learners to critically reflect on their thinking and actions, as well as on alternative approaches and choices. They can allow learners to at least hold onto doubt for longer and seek out other possible versions, helping to reinforce understanding that there is usually more than one possible interpretation or approach to a complex situation, and that there is often no 'right answer' or 'right way' to do something in professional practice. They can also help develop the type of reasoning, deliberation and judgement needed to deal with the complexity of practice.

Supervision, mentoring and coaching all use learning through experience and critical reflection (explored in the previous chapter) as key development tools (Brockbank and McGill, 2002), and they all rely on dialogue and questioning as a means of enabling learning.

Dialogue – the role of critical questioning

Dialogue, and in particular critical questioning, is a fundamental part of coaching, mentoring and supervision. Recent research shows that practitioners value 'continuous conversations' in 'learning workplaces' for their professional development (Beddoe, 2009).

The role of discussion and questioning was discussed in the previous chapter when we considered how best to enable deeper reflective learning. The aim was to move beyond description to more meaningful analysis and evaluation. McGill and Beaty (1995) recommend the use of questions that are open (e.g. how...? why...?), affective (e.g. how are you feeling?) and probing/checking (e.g. when...? where...? in what way...?). Remember, there are no 'right' questions to ask learners because there are no clear-cut answers. 'Certain' reasons and justifications are not always appropriate when talking about professional knowledge. In fact, as with many conversational situations that aim to enable learning and development, success depends on listening correctly too (i.e. actively, without interruption or judgement) and on reflecting back what you think you have heard for clarification.

Critical questioning (Brookfield, 1987) takes the dialogue process one step further in drawing out not only assumptions and underlying thoughts but also personal givens and accepted public truths. Questioning someone to elicit self-scrutiny of such issues must not become, or be seen as, behaviour that insults, threatens or attacks their self-esteem. As we now know, it is not what you do as an educator but how learners perceive that action which will lead to their response. If learners perceive your questioning techniques as threatening in any way, they will retreat or attack, and the learning experience will become a negative situation.

Critical questioning therefore involves very skilful framing of insightful and empathetic questions to encourage analysis and challenge thinking. This is a skill that may need training and subsequent practice and refinement for educators but many skills may be transferred from the type of work undertaken already with service users. Brookfield (1987, pp 93–4) suggests general guidelines including:

- *be specific* – relate questions to particular events, situations, people and actions;
- *work from the particular to the general* – exploring a general theme within the context of a specific event helps people feel they are in familiar territory;
- *be conversational* – informal, non-threatening tones help people feel comfortable.

We would add another suggestion: be aware of the effect your questioning is having and watch for any negative signs, such as non-response, a defensive position being argued too aggressively, brooding resignation.

We can now explore coaching, mentoring and supervision in turn to show the particular approaches, techniques and methods of each. Of course, we can present only overall ideas here but you can use the further reading lists to explore these methods in more detail.

Coaching

There are a number of circumstances where short-term coaching can help people to be more effective in their roles. For example, we all know workers who qualified many years ago and are stuck in habitual ways of working. For instance, John has become fixed on using a task-centred approach and he says it has 'done him well' over the years. Coaching can help to challenge John's habitual thoughts and actions by allowing him to safely explore and evaluate alternative approaches away from people he knows. Coaching is not necessarily provided by someone who is an expert in the subject, but rather by someone who has an expertise in coaching techniques. If you were John's coach and from a different department from him, you could easily play devil's advocate in your discussions, getting John to re-examine some more fundamental issues, and thus increase John's capability to think more flexibly.

Coaching is not about telling someone how to do their job. Any teaching and advice are generally aimed at developing the person's skills, knowledge and confidence to enable them to find their own solutions. You would not be 'judging' John's practice or telling him how to adopt a different social work method. One of the fundamental tenets of coaching is that the person being coached is the 'expert' in their subject or practice area and has the capability to achieve their goals with the support of the coach. You would be developing John's confidence and motivation to look more openly at other practice approaches. This should be a very non-threatening learning environment, and for John it could mean some very transformative learning.

Coaching is therefore a deductive process, one of 'drawing out' the necessary change or development from the person being coached, helping them to learn, enabling them to be more analytical, think more critically and problem-solve more effectively. The remit of a coach, however, is quite narrow. Coaching is most commonly time-limited, a one-to-one process which is set up to enable the person being coached to achieve specific goals or targets; it focuses on results and how those results can be most effectively achieved. It is often about supporting change and helping people to move on, so when it is done well it is a very empowering technique.

These are some methods used in coaching.

- Challenging assumptions, prejudices and habitual thinking.
- Supporting problem-solving and decision-making.
- Supporting metacognitive development (skills such as learning how to learn, improving critical thinking, etc.).
- Enabling people to recognise and empathise with other perspectives.
- Enabling the transfer of learning/skills/knowledge from one situation to another.
- Negotiating, agreeing and monitoring achievement of objectives.
- Identifying the need for new learning.
- Planning and facilitating the new learning.

Mentoring

Mentoring is generally considered to have a wider remit than coaching. Mentors are often provided for newly qualified workers or workers taking on new areas of responsibility to help them develop the specific skills and knowledge required to undertake their new role. Although mentors are always more experienced members of staff than mentees, the mentor relationship should not be hierarchical. It is sometimes described as a 'learning alliance' to demonstrate that the relationship is about working in partnership to support learning, principally of the mentee but also of the mentor (Thompson, 2006).

One of the most significant differences between coaching and mentoring is that mentoring should always be provided by someone who is skilled and experienced in the mentee's field of work and is able to provide direct support with the development of knowledge, skills and confidence (Neary, 2000; Mullins, 2005). Familiarity with the mentee's work environment is also very important. Mentor arrangements are normally longer term than coaching relationships and will often involve more frequent contact, including access to the mentor's support in between any formal mentor sessions that take place. The objectives for the relationship are likely to evolve over time as the mentee develops skills and confidence and shifts their focus from one area of their practice to another.

These are some methods used in mentoring.

- Direct teaching through the provision of information.
- Clarification and explanation of policies, procedures and legislation.
- Working through case studies to develop understanding.
- Sharing material such as reports and records to help the mentee understand the organisation's requirements.
- Shadowing by the mentee of the mentor's work.
- Joint working to aid the development of skills and confidence.
- Reflective discussions in mentor sessions.
- Objective setting.
- Recommendations for reading and research.
- Setting of learning and development tasks.

CASE STUDY *8.1*

A newly qualified social worker, Beth, makes a routine home visit to a long-term service user of the agency at the request of the regular worker who has been called away

continued

urgently. *Although the service user is told that Beth will be coming, he refuses to open the door to her but shouts through the window and tells her in no uncertain terms to get lost. Beth is very upset at the incident – she describes anger, frustration, helplessness and embarrassment. Ali, her mentor, thinks of some questions which may help Beth move on from her feelings and uncomfortable position in the situation to examine broader issues regarding her own practice and why the situation might have occurred. Ali knows the importance of examining case notes thoroughly before any visit to understand what might be going in a service user's mind (e.g. suspicion, privacy issues) and can see why this service user may well have reacted in the way he did. Ali gently leads Beth away from a negative emotional view of what happened by focusing his questions on key practices that Beth can easily improve on for more positive, future outcomes.*

Mentoring is a means of ensuring that knowledge and skills are passed from experienced members of staff to those who are less experienced, and can be an effective way of supporting a culture of learning within the workplace.

Supervision

The supervisor in an educational role supports in-depth exploration and analysis of work processes from their initial allocation through to completion of tasks, helping the supervisee to test their assessments, explore and uncover assumptions, prejudices, alternative perspectives and gaps in knowledge and consider alternative approaches.

According to Smith (1996, 2005) and Hawkins and Shohet (2000), supervisees may be helped to:

- understand the client better;
- become more aware of their own reactions and responses to the client;
- understand the dynamics of how they and their client are interacting;
- look at how they intervened and the consequences of their interventions;
- explore other ways of working with this and other similar client situations.

Effective supervisors can help learners reflect and gain an in-depth understanding of a situation and facilitate analysis to enable learning and decision-making processes. They can also encourage learners to adopt a more independent role and take responsibility for management and self-evaluation of their own learning during this process. These approaches support the development of more transferable skills, such as creativity, critical thinking, problem-solving and decision-making, which will enhance professional capability. As seen earlier, the right balance between supervisory authority and supervisee autonomy needs to be thought through for each individual learner.

A supervisor can also ensure there are effective learning outputs from the process. They can help learners to scaffold and integrate the knowledge and understanding that result from critical reflection and place it into a work-based context for future use. With these aims in mind, Davys and Beddoe's (2009, p932) reflective learning model might be used to provide *parameters, guidelines and information* in order for supervisees to *begin to construct their own sense of mastery of the skills and interventions required by practice*. The model describes four sequential stages that can be revisited at any time in the process: event, which involves description and clarification; exploration, which involves reflection of impact and evaluation of implications; experimentation, which concerns implementation or moving forward of ideas so they are not lost; and evaluation of the whole agenda.

Of course, supervision enables all levels of workers; in some situations younger staff may be supervising more experienced workers, or vice versa. Managing the various power and experience issues can be difficult to judge, but following the principle of working in partnership allows for a more egalitarian and humanistic approach, i.e. a supervisor does not need to adopt the role of an expert.

CASE STUDY 8.2

Velma is supervising Joan, an experienced worker. Velma's patience is being challenged by Joan's entrenched, negative views of young, unmarried mothers. Velma knows she has to question Joan in a very critical but sensitive manner so that Joan does not end up taking a defensive and negative position by feeling threatened or exposed. She also wants to avoid damaging their relationship. Velma knows there are many similarities between critical questioning and effective counselling skills. She endeavours to transfer these skills by thinking through ways to empower Joan to reflect and develop her own thinking on this issue. She needs a way in that is safe and unobtrusive and which does not set her up as the 'expert' or perfect social worker, which will only alienate Joan. She decides to discuss with Joan the course she recently attended, which had introduced the stages of knowing to her. She explains the ideas to Joan and professes to still being an 'absolute thinker' in many ways. Joan finds it difficult to believe this but Velma shares an example of how she feels so angry about male car mechanics who always seem to treat her with disdain, which then makes her believe they are all arrogant, brash young men out to rip her off. As the conversation develops, Joan begins to relay a story about a recent encounter she had with a teenager and her baby – this is the way in – together they unpick how and why their feelings and attitudes to certain others become so negative, and how they can try to remedy this.

These are some methods used in supervision.

- Case-work discussion.
- Critical questioning.
- Critical incident analysis.
- Role-play.
- Imagined scenario building.
- Reflective journals.

Enabling theory–practice connections and evidence-informed practice

Making connections between theory (and/or research) and practice is an important aspect for developing critical practice, and supervision is a perfect place for it to be enabled. The more traditional way is for the learner to consider theory first and then use it to explain or inform practice and predict the outcome. This view has been criticised (Margetson 2000, cited Nixon and Murr 2006, p807) as it can develop fixed 'templates' which do not fit more complex cases. More specific details or information about cases or service users may become ignored, or manipulated to fit theory, which distorts true understanding. For example, when working with children and applying attachment theory, it is important to recognise the limitations of its classifications and be aware that individuals who are securely attached can nevertheless display aspects of either avoidant or ambivalent behaviour.

We can see that theory and research findings can only inform; they cannot predict or control exactly what will take place. Research evidence can be extremely useful material for social workers (especially newly qualified) to gain more information about issues, possible interventions and outcomes, but it cannot be taken 'off the shelf' as an unmediated solution, or be seen to exactly 'match' a specific situation. In fact, it would be difficult to reduce the complex, uncertain and unstable situations we work with to something that a standardised theoretical body of knowledge, or a set of specific research findings, can answer (Adams, et al., 2002). To apply or base practice on any type of evidence without moral or ethical sensitivity, or a wider assessment of context, individual circumstances, situational requirements, or risk assessment of possible implications would be deemed 'uncritical' practice and is unacceptable (Brown and Rutter, 2008).

A learner can also undertake more inductive problem-solving where the detail of real situations is analysed first before looking at which theories or research findings relate to this. This enables learners to start to interpret practice, and in turn allows for complexity and creativity to be taken into account. (Note how neatly and effectively this fits with our notion of professional capability.) However, there are dangers here too. For example, when discussing particular cases it would be important not to become fixed on one set of prominent issues (e.g. behaviour), and then fail to notice other aspects (e.g. culture), which theory or research might show are significant.

As discussed earlier, a student or novice practitioner with less practical experience may want more direction and 'rules' to follow and look to more formal knowledge to provide it. This type of practitioner will need to be enabled to start reflecting on the practice situation first, i.e. to describe, analyse and evaluate the significant aspects for themselves and develop their professional judgement. Collingwood (2005; Collingwood, et al., 2008) provides some practical ideas for use in supervision which encourage theory–practice integration.

A review of thinking in this area (Nixon and Murr, 2006) concludes that professional knowledge is created by combining and recombining more explicit formal knowledge with an understanding of tacit knowledge from professional processes. Kondrat (1992) talks about the practitioner being able to move from the subjective perspective to an objective view of that perspective and back again. Consequently both deductive and inductive reasoning are likely to be taking place and the fundamental need for professional judgement and evaluation is an essential part of both processes.

Bringing it all together

ACTIVITY 8.2

Think about your learner – the type of learner they are and what they need to learn. Consider a range of relevant learning theories and how they can inform your understanding and your ideas. You are aiming for deep, reflective, experiential learning. You want this learner to critically analyse and evaluate their practice, i.e. to think about different perspectives on the situation they are working in and to critically explore a number of different approaches they could have taken. Briefly design/map out an appropriate range of learning opportunities – be creative!

Comment

By creating tailored learning opportunities which allow learners to approach their learning in active, questioning and critically reflective ways, you should be enabling the development or the enhancement of critical practice.

Of course, you also play a key role in all these learning situations not only by ensuring that learners have access to a wide range of practice experience and opportunities to critically discuss and reflect on their own practice, but by modelling a critical, reflective approach to practice as well. Part Four will look at this in more detail by considering your continuing professional development, but before then Part Three will focus on managing the assessment of learning.

Summary of Part Two Domain B

- The key guiding principles for enabling work-based learning are: establishing an effective working relationship and partnership with the learner; valuing the learner's perspective and adult learning principles; following an aligned approach.

- The main areas involve understanding the learner, developing learning objectives, considering learning theories and designing appropriate learning opportunities.

- It is important to review the learning schemes you design, involve the learner and link to how well they are doing – be flexible; adapt and change if necessary.

- There is no one overall definition of 'learning'; it is a very complex and situated phenomenon.

- Work-based learning activities should encourage learners to critically reflect on, analyse and evaluate their practice as well as provide opportunities to explore alternative approaches wherever possible.

- The reflective process should be active, holistic and meaningful, and critical.

- Coaching, mentoring and supervision all provide ways to develop critical practice through dialogue and questioning.

FURTHER READING

Brockbank, A and McGill, I (2002) *Facilitating reflective learning through mentoring and coaching.* Kogan Page: London.
Provides background information together with a helpful section on practice skills.

Cartney, P (2000) Adult learning styles: Implications for practice teaching in social work. *Social Work Education*, 19 (6), 609–626.
A practical and also critical look at using learning styles in social work practice education.

Doel, M and Shardlow, S (1998) *The new social work practice: Exercises and activities for training and developing social workers.* Aldershot: Arena.
This book offers very creative ideas to think about and some excellent practice learning activities.

Fook, J and Gardner, F (2007) *Practising critical reflection. A resource handbook.* Maidenhead: Open University Press and McGraw-Hill Education.
An in-depth look at critical reflection in practice, offering skills, strategies and tools for personal and educational use.

Kadushin, A and Harkness, D (2002) *Supervision in social work.* 4th edition. New York: Columbia University Press.
A basic text covering the challenges of supervision; for social work educators, practitioners, supervisors and agencies.

Part Three
Domain C: Manage the assessment of learners in practice

Meeting the requirements of the Practice Educator Professional Standards (CSW, 2012)

The material in this part links to the following domain standards.

Domain C: Manage the assessment of learners in practice

Practice educators at Stages 1 and 2 should:

1. Engage learners in the design, planning and implementation of the assessment tasks.

2. Agree and review a plan and methods for assessing learners' performance against agreed criteria.

3. Ensure that assessment decisions are the outcomes of informed, evidence-based judgements and clearly explain them to learners.

4. Evaluate evidence for its relevance, validity, reliability, sufficiency and authenticity according to the agreed standard.

5. Use direct observation of learners in practice to assess performance.

6. Base assessment decisions on all relevant evidence and from a range of sources, resolving any inconsistencies in the evidence available.

7. Encourage learners to self-evaluate and seek service users', carers' and peer group feedback on their performance.

8. Provide timely, honest and constructive feedback on learners' performance in an appropriate format. Review their progress through the assessment process, distinguishing between formative and summative assessment.

9. Make clear to learners how they may improve their performance. Identify any specific learning outcomes not yet demonstrated and the next steps. If necessary, arrange appropriate additional assessment activity to enable them to meet the standard.

10. Ensure that all assessment decisions, and the supporting evidence, are documented and recorded according to the required standard. Produce assessment reports which provide clear evidence for decisions.

11. Ensure that disagreements about assessment judgements and complaints made about the assessment process are managed in accordance with agreed procedures.

12. Seek feedback from learners on their experience of being assessed, and the consequences of the assessment programme for them. Incorporate the feedback into future assessment activity.

13. Contribute to standardisation arrangements and the agreed quality-assurance processes which monitor the organisation's training strategy.

14. Using professional judgement and drawing on appropriate support, demonstrate the ability to make difficult assessment decisions around areas of development, which may include marginal or failing students.

> **Additional learning outcomes for practice educators at Stage 2**
>
> 1. Where appropriate and drawing on support, demonstrate the ability to mark students' academic work.
>
> 2. Demonstrate an ability to use a range of assessment methods including recording, reports and the feedback of people who use services and carers, professionals and other colleagues.

Introduction to Domain C

We have already established that becoming – and indeed remaining – an effective social worker is not a simple process. Social work practice is a challenging activity that must be underpinned by an understanding of the complex relationship between knowing, acting and being, described by Barnett and Coate (2005) as professional capability. In Parts One and Two we looked at how practice educators can facilitate learning to support the development of processional capability and in Part Three we will move on to consider the challenging subject of how social work practice can be assessed. As part of this discussion we will introduce and discuss the concept of holistic assessment and show how the newly introduced Professional Capabilities Framework (CSW, 2012) can be used to benchmark performance at different stages of a social work career.

When asked to reflect on early experiences of making assessment judgements in a professional context, most people recall feelings of uncertainty and anxiety. It is not uncommon for even the most confident of social workers to experience similar feelings when faced with the responsibility of assessing a student for the first time.

Practice educators are often called the gatekeepers for the profession because they have an important role to play in deciding whether or not students and newly qualified social workers are able to move on to the next stage of their career (Lafrance, et al., 2004). This can quite reasonably feel like a heavy responsibility, as preventing the progress of people who have already invested large amounts of time and money is not something to be taken lightly, while passing someone who could be a danger to service users is obviously unthinkable (Walker, et al., 2008).

This section of the book will provide information and ideas that will help develop your confidence in the assessment of learners. It will encourage you to evaluate your existing skills, knowledge and attributes and consider how these can be transferred and further developed to enable you to make holistic judgements that are fair, reliable and accurate. We will focus particularly on the assessment of social work students but many of the principles and strategies that you will encounter can be applied to the assessment of any learner in the workplace and will be particularly useful in work with NQSWs.

Part Three is divided into three chapters. Chapter 9 provides an introduction and overview to the assessment of learners in the workplace. It links back to earlier chapters and explores links between assessment and learning. Chapter 10 looks in more detail at the assessment process, breaking it down into seven stages. Chapter 11 provides you with examples of specific tools that you can use to assess learners, and helps you to consider how you can use these strategies in your own workplace.

Chapter 9
Understanding the assessment of social work practice

So far in this book we have looked at what professional learning is and why the concept of capability is important when we are considering what social workers need to learn. In this chapter we will begin to explore the relationship between learning and assessment. This will give us a better understanding of the reasons why we assess and enable us to think more deeply about the wider role that assessment can play in the development of professional practice. We will start by addressing the fundamental but deceptively simple question – why do we need to assess social work practice in the first place?

Why do we assess?

This appears to be a very straightforward question and is one we often ask at the beginning of assessment workshops. Responses generally fall into the following broad categories;

- to find out what learners know or what they can do;
- to judge whether or not learners are good enough to qualify or move on to the next stage of their learning;
- to give learners feedback on their learning and/or their practice;
- to give practice educators feedback on how effective their teaching has been.

These are all valid and important justifications for undertaking assessments, but they are not the only ones. If we look more deeply at the connections between learning and assessment we will see that the relationship between the two is far more complex than the above list suggests and that understanding this relationship is a fundamental prerequisite for effective teaching and assessment (Biggs, 2003).

RESEARCH SUMMARY **9.1**

It has been shown that what people learn is strongly influenced by the way that they think their learning will be assessed. Ramsden (1992) found that the primary goal for many learners was not the learning itself, but the achievement of a good assessment outcome. Because of this they tend to focus on the parts of their course that will help them do well in their assessment tasks – often to the detriment of other aspects of their learning.
Earlier research had already shown that the approach taken by learners could be influenced by the assessment strategies used by their teachers. Marton and Säljö (1976) found a clear link between the design of assessment tasks and the adoption of deep/

continued

MARY 9.1 continued

...to learning (see Chapter 5 for more details on deep and surface ...3) investigated this link further and found that when students ...oach would enable them to do well in an assessment task (e.g. ...nt involved simple recall of facts) they were much more likely to adopt ...pproach. Conversely when an assessment task was designed to test for deeper ...ning (e.g. seeking to establish levels of understanding or the ability to transfer knowledge and understanding from one context to another), students would more frequently adopt a deep approach to their studies.

It would seem, therefore, that assessment is not simply a tool for measuring achievement and providing feedback about performance but an integral part of the learning process, with the power to exert a great deal of influence over what and how people learn. Badly designed and inappropriate assessment strategies have repeatedly been shown to skew learning and change priorities towards what will be assessed rather than what actually needs to be learnt (Singh, 2001). By contrast, well-designed assessment strategies not only enable learners to demonstrate their achievements but also ensure that learners' attention is directed towards fully meeting their intended learning outcomes. So, we can see that in order to give a more accurate description of why we assess we need to add a further principle to the above list:

- to direct and shape learning – by helping learners to understand exactly what they need to learn and how they can demonstrate achievement of their objectives.

In the following case study we will show how assessment can influence the depth of learning achieved in a practice situation.

CASE STUDY 9.1

Jenny and David are social work students in the early stages of their placements in the same busy children and family team. As part of their induction their practice educators decide they need to understand how Attachment Theory (Bowlby, 1969) informs the team's approach to practice.

Both students are given books and articles to read together with the opportunity to shadow an experienced worker undertaking an initial assessment. Individual follow-up supervision sessions are arranged to provide an opportunity for their practice educators to assess the learning that they have achieved.

Both practice educators give clear information to the students about how their learning will be assessed before they embark on their learning experience:

- Jenny's practice educator tells her that in her follow-up supervision session they will be doing a short quiz about Attachment Theory to enable Jenny to demonstrate her knowledge and understanding of the theory.

- David's practice educator explains that in his follow-up supervision session they will discuss what David had learnt from his reading and his shadowing opportunity. She asks him to bring his reflective notes to the session to help him critically explore how he believes Attachment Theory has informed the experienced worker's practice.

continued

CASE STUDY 9.1 *continued*

The two students have good academic records and have both already demonstrated to their practice educators that they are naturally reflective practitioners. However, clear differences emerge in the way that David and Jenny approach this particular learning task.

To succeed in her quiz Jenny realises she simply needs to learn some basic facts about Attachment Theory. She meets this learning objective the day after the task is set by memorising key ideas, significant dates and research data from the resources she had been given by her practice educator. Although she observes an experienced worker undertaking an initial assessment she doesn't link the observation with Attachment Theory in the way that her practice educator intends. She hurries away after the observation without discussing what she has seen and although she later makes notes in her reflective diary, they are about about procedural issues relating to the assessment, with no specific mention of attachment issues or Attachment Theory.

David, by contrast, is forced to take a different approach to his learning because he knows to succeed in his assessment task he needs to demonstrate an understanding of how theory can inform practice. David reads the material he has been given but he doesn't spend much time memorising facts. Instead, he notes questions to ask before the shadowing experience to help him understand more about Attachment Theory and how and when it is likely to be used in the intervention. During the observation David focuses mainly on the areas of practice that the worker has indicated will be most relevant to his learning and afterwards asks more questions to ensure that he understands what he has observed. David's reflective diary entry is sharply focused and includes a detailed analysis of both his observations and his discussions with the worker. David is able to make clear links between theory and practice and is also beginning to think about some alternative theories that could have been useful in the intervention he has observed.

Despite the differences in approach, the students perform well in their respective assessment tasks. As a consequence both practice educators are satisfied that they have enabled the students to learn about Attachment Theory and feel justified in making positive comments in their final reports about knowledge relevant to practice.

In Case Study 9.1 we have just considered, it is undeniably true that (a) both students have been enabled to learn about aspects of Attachment Theory, and that (b) both have provided evidence that can be used as part of their overall assessment. But, it is worth pausing to consider what has actually been achieved by David and Jenny and to review the links between their learning and assessment.

Although both David and Jenny were set the same objective and were offered similar opportunities, they chose to use the opportunities differently. Because the students wanted to impress their practice educators and be successful in their placements, it seems likely, based on the research evidence we considered earlier, that the assessment strategies adopted played a role in influencing the learning decisions that they made. Jenny appears to have been driven towards surface learning – with a focus on gaining superficial knowledge and understanding – whilst the more complex and demanding assessment strategy adopted by David's practice educator appears to have encouraged and supported much deeper learning to take place. This will almost certainly have led to very significant differences in the learning outcomes for the two students, with David in a much stronger position to use his learning to inform his own future practice.

However, it is not just the learning outcomes that are different. The differences in the assessment strategies adopted also mean that the quality of assessment evidence available to the practice educators varies widely. Jenny's assessment task has only generated evidence of her knowledge and understanding of one specific theory whilst David's practice educator has far more evidence to draw on. He is able to assess not only David's knowledge of Attachment Theory but also David's ability to critically use his knowledge to analyse and inform practice. And because of the approach that the assessment strategy encouraged towards learning, he will also be able to make some judgements about David's wider capabilities, for instance his ability to take professional responsibility for his own learning, communicate with other professionals and use supervision effectively.

The concept of professional capability

So now we need to begin to bring some ideas together and think about how they can help us understand more about the development and assessment of professional capability. In Chapter 1 we introduced the concept of professional capability and discussed some of the reasons why the Professional Capabilities Framework (PCF) (CSW, 2012) has been developed as a benchmark for social work practice. We looked at the fact that social work is a complex activity and considered how the introduction of the PCF attempts to capture that complexity and provide practice educators, assessors and managers with a tool that can be used to guide learning and judge performance both in initial social work education and in continuing professional development.

Case Study 9.1 shows just how important it is to use assessment strategies that shape the 'right sort' of learning (deeper learning) and enable us to measure professional performance effectively. The College of Social Work hopes that the PCF will accomplish both of these objectives by offering a framework that not only sets out what social workers should be achieving at different stages in their careers but also provides guidance on how the complexity of the task can be captured and judged. Unlike the National Occupational Standards (TOPSS, 2002) that it replaces, the PCF does not just focus on the component parts of practice but encourages educators to take into account the way that those parts are brought together to form professional expertise. This is a very important step forward in social work education because for the first time there is formal recognition that an over-simplified assessment system not only fails to measure practice capability but can actually drive social workers to develop a fragmented view of their practice that inadequately prepares them for their complex role in society.

In the final part of this chapter we move on to look at holistic assessment – the approach to assessment that is being promoted by the College of Social Work for measuring professional expertise (CSW, 2012).

What is holistic assessment?

Holistic assessment is not a new idea in social work – it is a process that most workers will be very familiar with from their assessments of service users and carers. In an educational context holistic assessment needs to be used in situations where learning or performance objectives are interrelated and complex. This clearly applies to the assessments that practice educators are now being asked to make against the nine domains of the Professional Capabilities Framework (PCF) in which the focus is not on making judgements about performance in individual elements of the framework but rather on measuring the development of professional expertise as a whole. Although the process of holistic assessment places a much greater emphasis on the professional judgement of the practice educator, it does not mean that these judgements are no longer required to be backed by evidence. The evidence required will, however, be different as it will need to show how social workers bring their skills, knowledge and values together across the domains rather than being linked to individual elements within domains.

One of the fundamental principles of holistic approaches to complex work contexts is that there is rarely a single 'right' way to practise. In every social worker's 'toolbox' there will be a wide range of 'tools' in the form of skills, knowledge and values and each time the worker reaches into that box to undertake a piece of work they make a decision (conscious or unconscious) about which combination of tools they think will work most effectively for them in that particular context. Two different workers approaching similar tasks may choose a different combination of tools and will almost certainly use the tools that they do select quite differently. However, despite the differences both practitioners could be equally effective in terms of the process and outcomes of their work. Because of these wide-ranging differences in the approaches that effective practitioners can take and the complex interactions between different elements of practice, it is important that the people assessing practice develop skills in judging the whole of practice and not just the component parts. To more fully capture practice capability it is also important to undertake holistic assessment over a period of time – judging performance not just on the basis of one piece of practice but on practice across a range of contexts and with different types of service users. This will enable judgements to be made about the transferability of skills and knowledge – including into untaught situations.

At the beginning of a professional career a worker's toolbox is fairly empty and their lack of experience means that it can be hard for them to know which tools to use and how to use them. With time, experience, education and support, professionals gradually add (and remove) tools to and from their boxes and become more confident in their ability to use them to approach complex tasks. This process of growth is sometimes described as the development of professional expertise and it is this overarching capacity to undertake professional tasks effectively that practice educators need to attempt to measure through holistic assessment. Because this capacity develops throughout a career it is clearly inappropriate to attempt to use a single set of standards to measure social workers at different stages of their development. It is therefore important that holistic assessment takes into account what could reasonably be expected at a specific stage of a social worker's career.

Although the main focus in holistic assessment is on taking an integrated approach, it would be wrong to suggest that there is never a need to look more deeply at specific aspects of a social worker's practice. At times practice may fall short of expectations and under such circumstances it can be useful to look at the component parts of practice as well as the practice as a whole. The individual capability statements that make up the domains of the PCF can help practice educators to drill down into practice, identifying gaps and areas for development or concerns. In their guidance on holistic assessment the College of Social Work (2012) use the analogy of eating a meal in a restaurant. They suggest that we make a holistic judgement based on the overall taste, quality and presentation of the meal but point out that if we are unhappy with the final product we may want to look more closely at the details of the preparation and ingredients to see what could have been improved. This process of drilling down is explored further in Chapters 10 and 11.

Principles and conditions for holistic assessment against the PCF

The College of Social Work website contains a wide range of useful resources for practice educators undertaking holistic assessment. These include guidance sheets, pro-formas and case studies. The following principles are drawn from the College of Social Work guidance on holistic assessment (CSW, 2012):

- assessment is progressive over time;
- assessment must be consistent with the appropriate level descriptor;
- evidence must be sufficient and provide depth across all nine domains;
- the assessment process must be trustworthy, reliable and transparent;
- the learner will contribute evidence for assessment but the professional judgement of sufficiency must be made by an appropriately qualified practice educator.

In the remaining chapters of Part Three we will explore some of the practical challenges that you will face undertaking a holistic assessment and consider some of the approaches that you can adopt to ensure that you are able undertake your assessment role effectively and fairly.

Chapter 10
The assessment process

In the previous chapter we looked at why we assess and established that assessment is a complex process that is an integral part of learning. We introduced the PCF as a learning and assessment tool and discussed the importance of holistic assessment in social work. Although we established that most assessment against the PCF will be approached holistically, we identified that there would be times, for example when a social worker was failing to provide sufficient evidence of capability, when there would be a need to 'drill down' into their practice. We suggested that this process would involve looking at individual elements of the domains to enable the practitioner and their practice educator/supervisor to identify areas of concern or for further development.

In this chapter we will look at assessment in greater detail and explore the range of ideas and strategies that will help you tailor your approach to the needs of individual learners and specific assessment contexts. This will include some strategies relevant to assessing holistically and others more specifically aimed at 'drilling down' into practice. Although you will probably feel that some of the strategies presented are rather time-consuming (for instance the development of detailed assessment objectives and criteria), they are designed to enable you to undertake trustworthy, reliable and transparent assessments of practice capability (CSW, 2012). This is particularly important in situations where practice is marginal, failing or when a learner is in need of clear developmental guidance on a specific aspect of their practice. It can also be useful in situations where there is a difference in views (between practice educators or between a practice educator and a learner) about what is good enough practice. Although it is, of course, not feasible or even desirable to negotiate and agree detailed assessment objectives for every aspect of the practice you are assessing, the basic principles of good assessment set out within the chapter should still be widely applied.

1. Planning assessment

When a student comes to a placement or a NQSW starts in a new job, they will have very specific assessment requirements. The first step that you as practice educator need to take is to establish what those requirements are by talking to the learner and accessing any written guidance that may be available. Although you will probably have a very clear idea about what you think makes a good social worker, you need to ensure that any assessment decisions you make are based firmly on the relevant nationally agreed standards and that you follow local university policies and procedures (Walker, et al., 2008).

In Part One, we established the importance of encouraging and enabling learners to take responsibility for their own learning and suggested that effective partnership was one of the ways that this could be facilitated. Partnership working is particularly important in assessment as it enables you to address (but not solve) the inevitable power imbalance that results from your role as the learner's assessor (Walker, et al., 2008). By encouraging and supporting the learner to make decisions about how and when they are assessed, you will give them some control over the assessment process. This can be developed further by ensuring that you provide opportunities for self-assessment and establish and facilitate a right to reply to your assessment judgements. Ensuring that self-evaluation and the critical analysis of feedback received are an integral part of assessment will not only address power issues but also support the development of self-awareness and critical practice – essential components of professional capability (Barnett and Coate, 2005).

In most social work learning situations the learner will carry ultimate responsibility for ensuring that they provide all of the evidence needed by the end of their placement or learning experience. However, you will obviously need to work with them to ensure that you provide appropriate opportunities for assessment to be carried out. The planning and organisation of the assessment process should therefore be a shared responsibility between the learner and the practice educator (see Part One for more on planning and organisation and Part Two for planning learning activities).

2. Deciding what you need to measure

In simple terms, what you need to measure will always be determined by the learning objectives that you have agreed with the learner or have been specified for the learner by the course that they are undertaking. It is important that the assessment aligns with the learning objectives and that the process is transparent to all involved (Biggs, 2003). In Chapter 6 we looked in detail at how to develop learning objectives and explored the importance of tailoring the learning objectives to reflect what you know about the learner and the learning context. Doing so ensures that you develop learning objectives in partnership with the learner that are achievable, relevant to the learning context, are understood by the learner and reflect the stage of development that they have reached. For social work students and NQSWs the learning objectives developed are normally linked closely to the Professional Capabilities Framework (CSW, 2012).

Some key learning objectives for students will be negotiated and agreed at the start of the learning experience and these will guide the overall direction of the learning and holistic assessment that takes place. Because these key learning objectives provide a succinct summary of the learning that is expected in the placement as a whole, they can often be rather broad. Examples may include, for instance, *demonstrating that the student has met the PCF at an appropriate level* or has *developed a critical understanding of research relevant to the interventions offered by the placement agency*. As these objectives will normally be the basis of the holistic assessments that you will be making it is important that they are discussed in detail with the learner to ensure that you have a shared understanding of what you will be measuring. An important part of this discussion should involve going through the PCF and talking about how it relates to your particular practice context. You can do this by giving examples of work that they are likely to be doing and showing them how this work will enable you to assess capabilities in more than one domain of the PCF. Doing so will also help the learner understand the principles of holistic assessment because you can show them how the capabilities in the domains are interlinked and discuss with them how you will be assessing their overall capability rather than the individual elements that make up the domains.

The broad learning objectives discussed in the last paragraph are often not so helpful when you decide that there is a need to 'drill down' into a learner's practice to find out more about areas of concern or learning needs. In these circumstances you may need to negotiate and agree much more specific assessment objectives. These can be used to break larger learning objectives down into more manageable bite-sized chunks and to help learners understand exactly what will be expected of them when they are undertaking a specific task. This is following case study.

Leah is a final-year social work student and needs to demonstrate that she has me learning objective to recognise the factors that create or exacerbate risk to individuals, families or carers, to the public or to professionals, including yourself, and contribute to the assessment and management of risk (CSW, 2012). She has agreed with Arvind, her practice educator, that she could demonstrate that she has met this learning objective through her work with Mr and Mrs Smith, who are both 93 years old and are currently living in their own home with some support from their daughter, Jane. Jane is worried about the risks faced by her parents at home and wants them to consider a move to sheltered accommodation. Mr and Mrs Smith have always said that they want to stay in their own home and Jane finds it difficult to express her concerns to them.

Arvind plans to directly observe Leah in a meeting with Mr and Mrs Smith and their daughter Jane. Arvind and Leah have discussed Leah's proposed approach to the meeting and as a result have jointly drawn up a list of specific objectives that Arvind can use to assess her performance.

During the meeting Leah will:
- *provide an opportunity for Jane to honestly and openly express her concerns to her parents and identify the exact nature of the risks she feels that they are facing;*
- *accurately and clearly summarise Jane's concerns and check that Mr and Mrs Smith understand why she is so worried;*
- *provide Mr and Mrs Smith with the opportunity to honestly and openly express their perception of the risks and benefits associated with staying at home;*
- *accurately and clearly summarise Mr and Mrs Smith's views and check that Jane understands their views;*
- *propose an action plan which includes an independent assessment of risk by an occupational therapist.*

These specific objectives enable Leah to understand exactly what she needs to do in the context of this current case to meet some of the PCF. They will also help Arvind to focus on specific and agreed aspects of Leah's practice.

3. Deciding how to measure it

Now we have established how to decide what we need to measure, we will consider how we can measure it. We will not, at this point, look in detail at the tools or methods you will be using in your workplace to assess practice, as these will be considered in Chapter 11. Here, we will look at some views on what makes a good assessment and look at some tips for improving the quality of assessments that you will undertake. The standards for good assessment that we are about to explore will enable you to make more informed decisions about selecting and evaluating assessment methods and help you to judge the quality of the evidence you gather.

...iere are a number of definitions of good assessment designed to help assessors accurately and fairly measure a learner's performance (e.g. Brown, 2001; Singh, 2001; Doel, et al., 1996). The Practice Educator Professional Standards (CSW, 2012) requires practice educators to ensure that any assessment undertaken meets the following standards.

- Relevant
  Does the selected assessment strategy enable the learner to demonstrate achievement of their learning outcomes?

- Valid
  Does the evidence presented demonstrate competent practice that is appropriate to the particular requirement being assessed at the time?

- Reliable
  Will the same results be achieved if the learner was assessed again in the same situation? Will different students with similar levels of competence be assessed at the same level in similar assessment tasks? Will different assessors achieve the same assessment results? What are the sources of bias? Have any assumptions been made that cannot be justified?

- Sufficient
  Is the evidence drawn from a large enough sample to ensure accuracy (e.g. from a whole interview not just a brief conversation)? Evidence should not just come from a one-off event but should be drawn from several occasions across the placement showing that the skill or knowledge has been learnt and can be applied at different times and in different contexts.

- Authentic
  Is the evidence presented definitely the work of the individual being assessed? If joint working has been involved, the assessor should be aware of the level of support provided for the learner and how much of the work was actually done by the learner.

It is worth remembering that few assessment methods are flawless and it is particularly difficult to ensure good assessment in work-based learning situations where so many variables are outside the direct control of the practice educator and the learner. However, careful assessment design can minimise the inaccuracies and improve the quality of the outcome.

Ideas for practice

- Match the assessment method you choose with the learning objectives, content and teaching methods; this is called constructive alignment (Biggs, 1999; Brown, 2001).

- Increase the sample of any given assessment. This means making sure that you sample enough of the knowledge or skills you are assessing for you to be confident that the assessment you reach presents a true and accurate picture (Singh, 2001). Sample performance in different settings and on different days to avoid fluke assessment judgements.

- Use assessment methods that are appropriate for the learning objectives. For instance, if you want a learner to demonstrate that they have a particular skill such as communication, use a method such as direct observation that enables you to see the learner applying the skill rather than a method which will test theoretical knowledge of a skill (e.g. an assignment) or ability to reflect on their use of a skill (e.g. reflective log).

- Employ a range of different methods to increase fairness (learners may perform better in some types of assessment tasks than in others).

- Make sure that the level of achievement expected is appropriate and that objectives are achievable in the situation provided.

- When using less reliable methods, increase the number of assessments planned; for example, in direct work with service users where it is possible that the service user may not turn up for an appointment, ensure that more than one opportunity exists for the assessment to take place.

- Justify and record assessment judgements openly, with judgements based solely on the assessment criteria which were set in advance.

- Make sure that the results of the assessment can be accurately interpreted. You can do this by thinking carefully about the way that you word the learning objectives. For example, assessing a learner's 'good communication skills' would be much more subjective and difficult to judge than specifically assessing whether a learner was able to communicate a particular message to a service user and be understood. So when you agree with the learner what you will be looking for in the assessment, try to ensure that you set objectives which are clear and measurable and avoid objectives that rely wholly or largely on subjective judgement.

- Where possible, include assessment judgements of more than one practice educator.

- Get involved in training and moderation opportunities for practice as this will help you find out more about the standards that other practice educators are using.

4. Collecting evidence

Once you have decided what to measure and how to measure it, you need to start collecting evidence. The responsibility for collecting evidence is normally shared between the practice educator and the learner with others, such as colleagues, service users and carers making contributions to the process. Everyone involved in the collection of evidence should have a shared understanding of the learning objectives and agreed assessment criteria as this will ensure that all of those who are playing a role in collecting evidence will understand what evidence is sought and how that evidence will be judged.

If we return to the case study from earlier in this chapter, Arvind and Leah agreed that one of the learning objectives that Leah would be assessed against was to *provide an opportunity for Jane to honestly and openly express her concerns to her parents and identify the exact nature of the risks she feels that they are facing.*

Unless Leah and Arvind agree assessment criteria that explicitly set out what Arvind is expecting to see before the observation takes place, there is a danger that they may have a different understanding of what good-enough practice looks like.

Examples of assessment criteria in this situation could include the following.

- *Very poor/unacceptable practice.* Leah does not ask Jane in the meeting how she feels about the risks that her parents are facing and after the meeting claims that Jane obviously didn't have any concerns because she didn't raise them herself.

- *Poor practice.* Leah asks Jane to describe how she is feeling about risk but does not support her or provide any encouragement when her parents disagree with her views.

- *Good-enough practice.* Leah asks Jane to describe how she is feeling about risk and provides some limited support when her parents disagree by suggesting that her parents listen to everything she has to say before they have their say.

- *Good practice.* Leah talks to Jane before the meeting and helps her to identify the key points she wants to raise and the evidence that she has to support those points. She suggests that Jane writes down her points to help her remember them and give her confidence in the meeting. In the meeting Leah provides support to Jane by asking questions which encourage her to fully and honestly express her concerns.

ACTIVITY 10.1

Write some of your own assessment criteria for Leah's learning objective to provide an opportunity for Jane to honestly and openly express her concerns to her parents and identify the exact nature of the risks she feels that they are facing. Make sure you are particularly clear about where the border falls between pass and fail.
You could focus on body language or communication skills and think of what you would expect to see Leah do to demonstrate her competence in this area of practice.

Comment

There are many different assessment criteria that could be agreed. The focus of the criteria developed will depend on a number of factors including the specific nature of the work being undertaken and the individual needs of the learner (this could be based on a previous observation of their practice). The criteria you use can be individually tailored to reflect the specific learning needs of an individual student that you may have in mind.

Gathering negative indicators of capability

A capable practitioner is not just one who is able to demonstrate that they can 'do things' or 'know things'. Capability is also about a lack of incompetence (Sharp and Danbury, 1999). To gain a full picture of a learner's capabilities it is important that, alongside the evidence we are gathering about things they can do, we also gather negative indicators, in other words, we catalogue the things that they can't do or don't understand. This will help you to put the evidence of capability in the context of the learner's whole practice and enable you to reach an accurate and fair assessment judgement.

5. Judging or weighing the evidence

Finding a way to accurately assess professional competence in social work has been problematic and the approaches taken in recent years have been the source of a great deal of controversy. Despite several attempts to develop standards to use as benchmarks (e.g. CCETSW, 1995; TOPSS, 2002) there has been a lack of agreement in the profession about the degree to which these competence-based systems could accurately reflect the complexity of the social work task (Thompson 2005; Lymbery, 2009). The most recent system for assessing social work practice – the PCF (CSW, 2012) – has addressed some of these long-standing concerns, by

encouraging more holistic assessment against benchmarks that specify expectati
domains at nine different stages of a professional career. By doing so the fram
to capture the complex nature of social work and encourages the assessment of
between elements of capability as well as the elements themselves.

However, although the PCF enables more comprehensive benchmarking and provides a clearer assessment process than previous systems, making judgements about achievements in practice will still remain a challenge for practice educators. This is because of the high degree of subjectivity involved, leaving individuals with the responsibility of deciding 'what is good enough' in their own context. This is difficult for any practice educator, but will be particularly challenging for people who are taking responsibility for assessing learners for the first time.

We all have our own views about what a capable practitioner should look like, and in general terms the PCF now provides us with statements that we can use as benchmarks for each of the key stages of a social work career. But, do you feel confident that you can apply the PCF within your own work context and understand what is good enough in relation to the work that your organisation undertakes? And do you believe that the judgements you make about a learner's practice will be the same as those made by one of your colleagues or by an assessor from outside of your team? Shardlow (1989, cited Shardlow and Doel, 1996) showed that there were very wide variations in assessment judgements made of the same piece of practice by different practice educators. This is because the assessment of social work competence can never be measured scientifically as the people carrying out the assessment are not neutral and are unable to act as value-free collectors of evidence (Cowburn, et al., 2000).

Furthermore, many of the assessment methods available to work-based practice educators rely heavily on learners' self-evaluations, such as supervision discussions, reflective recording and assignments; or on evaluations carried out by service users. Such assessments are obviously highly subjective and therefore potentially unreliable or misleading (Shardlow and Doel, 1996).

To overcome some of the difficulties described above, Shardlow and Doel (1996) encourage practice educators to triangulate pieces of evidence. This suggestion is based on the hypothesis that when two or more pieces of evidence from different assessors, assessment methods or contexts correspond with each other, the more likely it is that an accurate assessment of practice has been reached. Triangulation therefore involves practice educators and learners working together to identify evidence from different sources (e.g. direct observation, self-assessment, feedback from a service user, feedback from colleagues) which all indicate the same thing in terms of the learner's competence in a particular area. When triangulation is carried out, assessment judgements are no longer based on the opinion of a single individual or from a single event. The strength of evidence produced will therefore be increased and the practice educator can be more confident that their assessment judgement is both accurate and fair.

So, we have established that you will face a difficult task judging evidence that you gather but nevertheless it is something that will be a very important part of your role as a practice educator. Considering the following questions may help you to reach your judgements.

- What level is the student at with their development and what can you reasonably expect a learner at this stage of development to achieve in the specific area of competence (bear in mind previous experience of undertaking this type of work as well as the stage they have reached in their course)?

- How complex or challenging was the specific piece of work that the learner was undertaking at the time of the assessment – was this more or less challenging than a learner at their stage of development would normally expect to undertake? Do you need to make allowances for this in reaching your judgement?

- What impact did assessment anxiety or the assessment method have on the learner's performance? Do you need to take this into account or provide further opportunities for the learner to demonstrate competence?

- How good is the quality of each piece of the evidence you and other assessors have gathered – is it relevant, valid, reliable and sufficient?

- Has triangulation helped to confirm your assessment decision because the evidence agrees or are there disagreements between different pieces of evidence?

- If you have anomalous results, can you justify or explain them? Do some of the results need to be given greater emphasis than others; should some be disregarded?

- Where there is a disagreement between pieces of evidence, has the learner's performance improved over time and does the most recent evidence demonstrate competence at a good-enough standard? Will you need further evidence or are you confident that performance has reliably improved in this area?

The nature of the assessment task that you will be facing is complex and highly dependent on the local circumstances of the learning experience you have provided. For example, a social work student working in a day centre for older people might be expected to take responsibility for planning and running activity groups in order to demonstrate their capability. However, a similar student working in a drug rehabilitation programme might not be expected to take the same level of responsibility in therapeutic groups because of the complex nature of the facilitator's role. In the second case, capability would be demonstrated through fulfilling an appropriate support role in the group and by demonstrating a clear understanding of the processes involved.

So you can see that the question *What is good enough?* cannot be answered in simple terms. One of the ways that you will develop your confidence about answering the question is through discussion with others, either through a support group for practice educators or by working with a mentor. Through discussion, you will be able to define minimum standards of practice in your own situation.

REFLECTION POINT

What opportunities already exist for you to discuss standards with other practice educators or a mentor?

If opportunities are currently limited, what will you do to ensure that you create opportunities to support your role?

6. Discussing the evidence with the learner and providing feedback

Throughout this book we have stressed the importance of working in partnership with learners to ensure that where possible they take responsibility for their own learning, and have established that their central involvement in assessment is a logical extension of this process.

Many supporters of reflective learning see self-assessment as a core skill in the development of professional practice and as an important part of the wider assessment process (Barnett and Coate, 2005; Knott and Scragg, 2010).

> We cannot expect students to become competent professionals unless they learn to be actively involved in constructing and reconstructing notions of good practice as they proceed.

(Boud, 1999, p122)

Including self-assessment as part of an assessment strategy and openly discussing assessment decisions with them helps learners to develop skills in making critical judgements about their own performance and encourages them to take more control and responsibility for their own learning (Crisp, et al., 2006). Self-assessment should not therefore be considered an alternative assessment method but should be an integral part of most other assessment methods (Cree, 2000, p30). For instance, you can encourage a learner to self-assess their practice after you have observed their practice, or to self-assess a letter sent to a service user. In such situations, the self-assessment will be part of the overall learning and assessment process, allowing both learners' and practice educators' perspectives to be incorporated into assessment judgements.

Despite the potential value of self-assessment, there are a number of problems with its use in practice. Learners can lack the self-assessment skills required to make meaningful contributions, may not have the expert knowledge needed to assess their practice (particularly at the early stages of learning) and can feel resentful that they are being asked to do the assessor's job (Boud, 1999). You may need to provide support to the learner to build the skills and confidence they need to enable them to actively engage in meaningful self-evaluation. You will also need to help them understand the breadth and depth of analysis and evaluation that are appropriate.

The learner needs to learn how to:

- ask themselves challenging questions;
- critically appraise new information;
- identify their knowledge and skill gaps;
- compare their actual performance with the standard required for the outcome and be able to take action to close the gap.

Modelling critical reflection and self-evaluation in your own practice may significantly assist learners with this process.

Discussing the evidence you are drawing on with the learner before you reach an overall decision about their capability is not only a good idea from adult and professional learning perspectives, but also makes sense if we want to ensure that our assessment would stand up to scrutiny if judged against the standards for good assessment outlined earlier in this chapter. This is because:

- you will see only snapshots of the learner's practice – the learner can help you understand more about the context and the reasons why they have taken a particular approach;

- your judgements are subjective and the learner will have a different perspective – you need to understand how they perceive the situation in which they are practising as a check to your own interpretations and judgements;

- you will find out more about the learner's feelings, anxieties, perceptions of the task they have been given and the context in which they are working and how this may have impacted on their performance;

- you will be able to gauge the learner's levels of self-awareness about their performance – they may have made some mistakes, but if they can identify the mistakes for themselves and are clear about how they would do things differently next time, your overall assessment would be more positive than one you might make about someone who was not able to see that something had gone wrong;

- you can check that if you and the learner have been working to the same learning objectives and assessment criteria – this may help if there is a mismatch between your assessment and the learner's self-assessment.

So, we have established that encouraging and supporting self-assessment is an important part of discussions with learners about evidence gathered but it is of course only half of the story. Feedback from experienced practitioners, including from you in your practice educator role, is an essential part of the learning process and will help to shape learning and provide detailed feedback on the evidence you have gathered from assessment activities. One of the key skills to develop in your practice education role is the ability to give feedback in a way that actively supports learning and development.

Feedback is the process of relaying to a person your observations, impressions, feelings or other evaluative information about that person's behaviour for their use and learning.

(Ford and Jones, 1987, p74)

The processes of assessment can generate feedback information that can be used by learners to enhance learning and achievement. Good-quality feedback on performance should therefore have a central role in aligned learning, teaching and assessment strategies. If learners are going to make use of feedback for development they should:

- know what standard they are aiming for (clear and agreed assessment criteria);
- be able to compare what they have achieved with the standard they are aiming at;
- understand what they need to do to close the gap and achieve the required standard (Sadler, 1989, cited Juwah, et al., 2004).

Providing good-quality feedback will empower learners to take control of their own learning. However, it is not enough to simply tell learners about the strengths and weaknesses of their work and hope that they will be able to understand how to use the information for development. Try to help learners to work out how they can make use of the feedback and bridge the gap between what they are currently achieving and what is expected.

As stated in Part Two, if you have a thorough understanding of what someone will be able to do as a result of their learning (learning objectives), then you can effectively plan to help someone achieve it. More importantly, by knowing how well you need it to be done (assessment criteria), you and they will be able to tell more accurately if and when they are achieving it.

Good-quality feedback, both positive and negative, maintains self-esteem and provides learners with choice. Destructive feedback leaves learners feeling demotivated, with nothing to build on. There is always an element of nervousness about giving and receiving feedback but it can be lessened if there is a shared intent and awareness that it may be a creative process leading to personal and professional development by both sides.

Obviously the feedback should be helpful and understandable. It may have to tackle awkward or difficult areas. By concentrating on the practice issues/behaviour, the work or the learning outcomes (i.e. the tasks, processes) rather than the learner's personality, attributes or abilities, you should be able to avoid it becoming 'personal' (i.e. being seen as a criticism of the learner as a person).

For example, as lecturers marking an assignment we might say that *the text lacks a critical analysis of the main issues* rather than *you lack critical analysis*. By focusing on what is being produced it is much easier to see what extra input, skills or knowledge are needed to help develop that area of work. It is also less discriminatory – it does not assume that the person is or isn't something. In our example, the person may be very critically analytical in their practice; it is just that at this time they are unable to articulate it in their writing.

Principles of good feedback

- *Specific rather than general.*
- *Refers to behaviour rather than the person.*
- *Clear – one message at a time, not too much information.*
- *Provided promptly to minimise unnecessary stress.*
- *Comes quickly to the point, without losing the message.*
- *Descriptive rather than evaluative.*
- *Recognises positive aspects, but does not apologise for addressing negatives.*
- *Is confident.*
- *Consistent – check feedback has been understood.*
- *Appropriate – linked to criteria and competences.*
- *Recorded so that the learner can take the information away with them.*
- *Positive – this is the beginning of the solution.*

Adapted from Sharp and Danbury (1999)

ACTIVITY **10.2**

You have to give feedback to a learner who does not make eye contact with people when she is talking to them. What is wrong with the following statement? How can you improve it?
You look strange and distant when you are talking to people; no one likes people who can't make eye contact.

Comment

To complete this activity you need to think about how you can depersonalise this feedback – removing the focus from the learner and their characteristics and instead placing the focus on their practice at the time.

The design of any learning scheme is enhanced with planned and co-operative feedback facilities that encourage and support the learner to self-evaluate as well as receive feedback in a constructive manner, enabling the learner to extend their learning and build confidence in themselves on their route to becoming critically reflective practitioners.

7. Reaching and documenting an assessment decision

So far we have looked at how you can decide what needs to be assessed and explored ways in which you can assess aspects of practice We will now consider how you can bring the elements of assessment together to reach an overall assessment decision. In the case of a social work student or NSQW this will normally involve making a pass/fail decision. In doing so it is important that you refer to the specific guidance produced by the learner's programme and seek support if you are unsure about procedures or need advice with regard to your assessment decision. The guidance provided should clearly set out the expectations for learners with regard to meeting standards in each placement or practice learning situation.

Although you will need to have a general feel for overall progress at all times during the placement and will need to ensure that the learner keeps good records of progress towards meeting objectives, there are specific points where you and the learner will formally be required to bring evidence together to enable you to make judgements about performance. In the case of a social work student these will normally be:

- at the mid-point of the placement where you will probably need to provide an interim review;

- at the end of the placement when you will need to provide a final report and make a pass/fail recommendation.

Individual programme requirements will vary with regard to documenting and reporting final assessments. Many programmes now give the majority of the responsibility for documenting and evaluating evidence to the student, with the practice educator's role limited to supporting the student in the development of their portfolio of evidence and the provision of a brief summative report. However, it is very important that you bear in mind that if a student is failing or marginal, you will be required to justify your assessment decision with detailed references to specific evidence of lack of competence in relation to the PCF. For this reason supervision notes and written feedback provided to the learner should contain enough detail to allow you to draw evidence together and make specific references to examples from practice if required.

Although you will have taken the views of others, such as the learner, your colleagues, service users and carers, into account in your assessment journey, the responsibility for the final assessment decision will rest with you as the practice educator (CSW, 2012). However, even at this point the importance of partnership with the learner is still strong. If you have worked collaboratively throughout the placement, your assessment decision should hold no surprises for the learner. However, even at this stage you need to give the learner an opportunity to read and comment on your report. Many programmes will have a formal requirement for this to happen.

You should ensure that your assessment decisions are linked to the PCF or other relevant standards and can be supported by clear evidence either from the learner's portfolio or through examples that you provide from the placement experience. A balanced report will highlight both strengths and areas for future development. Don't shy away from highlighting these learning needs – they do not indicate a weak learner but rather provide an indication of a commitment to ongoing development.

The final report can emerge naturally out of an effective collaboration. Work with the learner and encourage them to highlight their most valued learning from the experience, their strengths and their development needs. If you agree, incorporate the learner's ideas into the report. If you disagree, base the report on your views but actively support the learner to honestly express their different views in their comments on your report. The report and the report development process are further opportunities for meaningful learning to emerge from the assessment process and form the end point of the seven stages of assessment.

In the next chapter we will look in greater depth at some of the methods that you can use to assess learners in the workplace.

Chapter 11

Assessing professional performance in the workplace

Assessing professional competence in the workplace requires a flexible and creative approach. As we have already discussed, the way that a learner is assessed will have a major impact on the quality and direction of their learning and it is therefore important to give careful consideration to the methods that you use to gather evidence and to reach judgements about practice competence. They should:

- be aligned with your intended learning outcome;
- be relevant, valid, reliable, sufficient and authentic;
- take into account your work environment, service users and the learner.

In this chapter we will explore a range of assessment methods that will enable you to gather evidence for holistic assessment – these methods could be considered as a 'starter-kit' for your practice educator's toolbox. The methods we consider are:

- supervision discussions;
- logs, diaries and reflective journals;
- critical incident analysis;
- case studies;
- projects;
- direct observation of practice;
- indirect or informal observation of practice;
- evidence from practice or from artefacts;
- feedback from service users;
- feedback from colleagues and other professionals.

Because of the limitations of space and our own creativity, this should not be considered a comprehensive list – as you gain more experience and confidence in your role you will adapt these methods and will be able to develop and explore alternative methods and approaches. All of the methods included here provide opportunities for enabling learners to play an active role in the assessment process and provide opportunities for assessing both competence and capability. As you read about the methods, think how you could maximise these opportunities and reflect on their relative strengths and weaknesses using the standards for good assessment provided in the previous chapter. As well as considering each method individually, you could consider how you could combine methods to triangulate evidence and overcome any weaknesses that you have identified.

Supervision discussions

Although supervision discussions have been described as the linchpin of prac
(Shardlow and Doel, 1996) and provide very useful evidence for holistic assessment, it ⌐
be remembered that any evidence is provided indirectly to the practice educator by the learner
themselves and is therefore selective and subjective (Singh, 2001).

Because evidence collection in supervision depends on the interaction between the practice
educator and the learner, you need to remember that the quality and quantity of assessment
information gained will be at least partially dependent on the reporting and reflective skills of
the learner. Assessment criteria should clearly allow separation of the judgement of these
transferable skills from the assessment of more specific practice competence. The practice
educator's skill as a facilitator is also relevant – skilled questioners will elicit more accurate
information (positive and or negative) than less skilled questioners. Skilled questioners are also
more likely to gain information about capability as well as competence by employing techniques that provide appropriate challenges to learners and enable judgements to be made about,
for instance, their depth and breadth of understanding and their ability to transfer their understanding to other contexts. In supervision you will be a key part of the learning environment
and will have a significant impact on the performance of the learner (Moon, 2002). You should
take these issues into account when you judge the evidence gained from supervision discussions.

Another issue with using supervision for assessment purposes is that because of the complexity
of many sessions, it would be impossible to agree assessment criteria for every aspect of the
discussions that could take place, making any assessment judgements reached open to criticism
on the basis of both fairness and accuracy (Shardlow and Doel, 1996).

Although some of the difficulties described above could be overcome by agreeing that supervision would not be used for summative assessment, this will not be a satisfactory solution to
the problem. Practice educators could not agree to disregard evidence of dangerous or
unsound practice disclosed in a supervision discussion. Therefore, while some assurances can
be provided that learners can openly discuss less-than-perfect aspects of their practice without
penalty, it is important that they understand that supervision discussions can and will be used
as a source of assessment material. A working agreement between the learner and practice
educator should be reached on how this will be managed, with a particular emphasis on the
limits that are set around confidentiality.

ACTIVITY 11.1

*You are planning to discuss a piece of legislation within a supervision session with a
social work student. You would like to use this discussion as evidence that the student
has a good understanding of how the legislation can be applied in practice for inclusion
in their final report. It should be possible for you to do so both fairly and accurately, but
what will you need to do before the session to make sure that this is the case?*

Comment

In order to make this a fair and accurate assessment you would need to consider agreeing
learning objectives and assessment criteria with the student before the supervision session

takes place. This would allow time for the student to prepare for the session and would ensure that you had a shared understanding of your expectations.

Logs, diaries, reflective journals

Reflective recording is widely accepted as a valuable learning and development tool in professional education (e.g. Brown and Rutter, 2008), but care is needed when you use reflective recordings for assessment purposes. Reflective recordings, like other indirect assessment methods, are inevitably highly subjective and can provide an incomplete picture of a situation. Learners select what they choose to include and what to leave out. Nevertheless, Moon (1999) believes that reflective material can be used for assessment purposes, as long as appropriate assessment criteria are agreed in advance between practice educators and learners. It is particularly important to be clear about whether it is the practice itself or the quality of the reflection on the practice that is being assessed when the criteria are set. Learners being assessed on the quality of their reflection can confidently record examples of their practice that need further development. However, learners who are being assessed purely on outcomes will not want to include less-than-perfect examples in their records.

Discuss the conflicts that arise from using reflective recording for assessment and learning openly with the learner from an early stage and agree how these will be managed. This may include sharing some, but not all, of the learner's reflective recording.

You can also stress the importance of the reflective recording for learning and provide reassurance about the way that you will interpret and evaluate the material included. For example, if the learner includes evidence of poor or weak practice alongside a clear analysis of what went wrong together with the steps they have taken to develop practice for the future, you would consider this to be positive evidence of their ability to critically analyse, evaluate situations and take responsibility for their own learning. Doing so will make it clear to the learner that poor or weak practice within a developmental context can provide valuable evidence of professional competence and capability. It may also be worth considering sharing some of your own reflective recordings to model good practice and demonstrate the importance of identifying areas for development.

Critical incident analysis

Critical incident analysis has been developed to enable social work learners to explore significant incidents from their practice experience and to use the learning from this exploration to inform future practice (Davies and Kinloch, 2000). Critical incident analyses can be completed either as specific pieces of reflective writing or as activities within supervision sessions and therefore the issues raised above in our explorations of supervision discussions and reflective recording are all relevant when considering the use of this assessment tool.

Critical incident analyses can be based on both positive and negative experiences, but should be used to explore situations in which significant learning has taken place. When asking learners to complete a critical incident analysis, you should ask for:

- a brief description of context;
- a description of what the learner did;
- an exploration of how theory influenced what the learner did and thought;
- an account of the outcomes of the intervention;

- what alternatives were considered and why they were rejected;
- how the learner would tackle the same incident differently on another occasion;
- what learning the learner took away and how it will influence their future practice.

ACTIVITY 11.2

Using the headings given above, write a critical incident analysis of an incident you were involved in during the last month. How could your analysis be used to assess your practice against the PCF?

Comment

Writing your own critical incident analysis will help you to be more confident using this method with others.

Case studies

Case studies can be used to enable learners to apply professional knowledge and understanding to specific material provided by the practice educator in a safe environment (often within supervision). Material for case studies can be written specifically by the practice educator or can be drawn from anonymised case records. It is even possible to use videos, soap operas or documentaries as sources of case study material as these often deal with some challenging scenarios and can bring case study work to life. Learners are presented with case material and are asked to work through it, analysing issues, making assessments and exploring solutions to presenting problems. This can be done either independently or in partnership with you or another experienced social worker.

This type of learning and assessment tool enables the learner to explore options, take risks and make mistakes with no danger to either themselves or service users. Through either a supervision discussion or the preparation of a written report, the learner can demonstrate the way that they would approach the case, apply theory to practice, take decisions, and so on. This can provide good material for assessment and may be particularly useful in deciding whether a learner is ready to take responsibility for working alone with service users.

Case study material can also be used to assess knowledge and understanding that cannot be directly tested in a particular learning environment; for instance, case studies that involve working with people with cultural backgrounds not generally encountered in a particular service.

As with other forms of assessment, if case studies are being used for assessment purposes it is important that there is a clear understanding between the practice educator and learner about what will be assessed, how it will be assessed (assessment criteria) and the purpose of the assessment (formative or summative). Because case study work does allow for safe experimentation, its most useful role is probably as a learning tool and a way of formatively assessing a learner's knowledge, skills and attributes. However, case studies can be used quite effectively as a way of summatively assessing knowledge and values that may be difficult to test in other ways.

It is worth considering that for a variety of reasons learners can perform very differently in a simulation such as a case study than they will in a real-life situation, so assessment evidence based on any form of simulation would ideally need to be triangulated with more direct forms of evidence.

ACTIVITY 11.3

Prepare a case study using some of the ideas above and think about how you would use this to assess a learner.

Comment

Having selected some material for use as a case study with the learner, you need to think about what learning objective the case study could help a learner meet and what assessment criteria you would use. How would you involve the learner in developing learning objectives and assessment criteria?

Projects

A project is a specific task that a learner is asked to complete, either on their own or in collaboration with others. Examples of projects sometimes given to qualifying students in placements include setting up new groups for service users or carers, undertaking consultations with service users, carrying out pieces of research such as feasibility studies, designing induction programmes and developing publicity materials for services.

Because projects can be quite time-consuming and can take on a life of their own, it is important that focus is maintained on the learner's overall learning objectives and that you and the learner clearly establish that they will be able to demonstrate appropriate achievement throughout the project. Assessment criteria should be agreed at the start of the project to enable the learner to understand how and when they will be judged. Particular care should be taken to establish whether the assessment will look at the outcomes of the project, the way that the outcomes were achieved, or the way that the project was evaluated by the learner – or a combination of all three.

Project work can give learners a degree of autonomy and provide an opportunity to see a piece of work through from beginning to end, but to be a relevant and reliable assessment method it is important to be sure that the project is feasible in terms of resources and achievable in the time available within the placement.

ACTIVITY 11.4

Can you think of any projects that a learner could undertake in your workplace? Which domains of the PCF would this project enable you to assess?

Comment

Consider developing a list of potential outline projects for discussion with students
learners as this would allow them to choose a project that matched their interests and lea.
needs. Link the projects to professional requirements that could be met through the project.
Think about how you could involve your team and service users and carers in this process.

Direct observation of practice

Direct and systematic observation is a requirement for learners on qualifying social work
courses and during the Assessed and Supported Year in Employment. Direct observation
involves a practice educator observing a learner carrying out a task, evaluating their performance and providing formal feedback (usually both verbally and in writing). Most universities
now provide guidance on how direct observations should be carried out and recorded. It is
therefore important that you ensure you are familiar with any requirements and use pro-formas
provided when appropriate.

Direct observation is one of the most powerful assessment tools in your toolbox because it is
one of the few methods in common use that does not rely on collecting indirect evidence. It can
also fit well with adult learning principles if learners retain responsibility for their own learning
by setting some of their learning objectives and assessment criteria and provide a detailed self-
evaluation of their achievements and learning after the observation has taken place (University
of York, 2000). Direct observation provides an opportunity for you to check a learner's perceptions of their practice by comparing your observations with their recollections. Direct
observation is therefore not only a powerful assessment tool but also an important part of
the learning process, both in terms of developing competence and professional capability.
However, do bear in mind that in social work there is rarely only one way to interpret a situation
or one right way to practise. Any observations you may make are therefore highly subjective
and need to be held up for critical scrutiny (Cowburn, et al., 2000).

Because a direct observation, even of a short piece of practice, will potentially generate an
enormous amount of data, it is a good idea to agree in advance some objectives and assessment criteria for the observation. Both the practice educator and the learner should contribute
to this process to ensure that the observation focuses on the learner's specific individual
learning needs and that both parties are clear about the standards required. Having clear
objectives and assessment criteria will enable the practice educator to focus on specific areas
of the practice and to write detailed notes on these areas during the observation. This will
enable the practice educator to provide good-quality feedback and to increase the accuracy
and fairness of the assessment judgement. It will also ensure that the learner has a clear focus
for their self-evaluation and is able to retain some control over their learning and assessment.

Direct observation of practice can provoke anxiety in some learners, which could have an
adverse impact on their performance. To ensure that this type of assessment is as fair and
accurate as possible, Doel, et al. (1996) suggest an approach to observation that is integrated
with learning. They say that, where possible, when observation is going to be used for assessment, practice educators should:

- discuss its use with learners at the pre-learning opportunity stage;
- discuss anxieties about the process openly;

- invite learners to observe their own practice (i.e., that of the practice educators) to build trust;
- evaluate their own practice openly with learners;
- enable the learner to move gradually from observer to participant to leader in practice situations as their confidence grows;
- undertake observations when the learner has reached an appropriate point of confidence and is used to taking the lead with the practice educator present.

Adapted from Doel, et al. (1996)

ACTIVITY 11.5

Ask a colleague to observe you making a telephone call/talking to a service user and to give you feedback on your practice against the PCF.

How did this make you feel? Did you get any unexpected feedback? Can you learn anything from the way that the feedback was given to you?

Comment

Having recent experience of being observed will help you to understand how someone you are assessing may be feeling. However, as people respond differently to assessment situations, don't assume that your learners will feel exactly the same as you do. Reflecting on receiving feedback will help you to develop your own skills in giving feedback to others.

One of the biggest problems faced by practice educators when observing practice is separating their role as an assessor from their role as a practitioner (Humphrey, 2007). It is very hard to stay outside of the practice and observe as if you were looking through a one-way mirror. Agree with your learner in advance what your role will be in the observation and if and when you will intervene. You need to take care not to contaminate the evidence by acting as a co-worker rather than as an observer (Humphrey, 2007).

Indirect or informal observation

Where practice educators are working alongside a learner, there will be many opportunities for informal observation and assessment of their practice. Although this will be a rich source of evidence, there are some dangers associated with this method of assessment. If we think back to the criteria given in Chapter 10 for good assessment, we can see that it is important for learners to be clear about when, where and how they are being assessed. It will obviously be difficult to be transparent about the assessment process if there are no clear assessment objectives and if observation is taking place all of the time. This could be overcome by agreeing in advance that informal observation will be used for assessment and by discussing with the learner particular objectives for observations at different stages of their learning and development. For instance, *This week I will be looking at your communication skills with service users.* You could then clearly set out the standards that you would be using in your assessment and agree some assessment criteria. The learner would then be aware that whenever you were in a position to observe them informally, you would be specifically looking at this area of their practice. You could provide feedback on your observations at agreed intervals and make clear links between your observations and assessment judgements (perhaps at supervision sessions).

Evidence from practice or artefacts

Learners can use material that they have produced as part of their professional practice for assessment purposes. Examples include letters, reports and assessments. It is particularly important when using this type of material to be clear about the assessment criteria used, because requirements and expectations may vary between workplaces and between workers. Samples of work produced by experienced workers could provide learners with instances of good-enough practice. Unless there is a prescribed format for a task, a range of examples by different workers should be used to provide the learner with an insight into some of the different approaches that can be taken.

ACTIVITY **11.6**

Write a list of criteria that you could use to assess a letter that a learner has written to introduce them to a new service user. The criteria should provide a clear statement of what you would be looking for from the letter (content, quality of writing, appropriateness of style for audience, etc.). This will help the learner to know exactly what you think is good enough. It will also help you to assess the letter fairly.

Comment

Some of the criteria will reflect organisational procedures and policies but others may reflect your own preferred approach to the task. Be wary about imposing a particular way of working on a learner when other approaches could work equally well.

Ideas for practice

This is another area where collaboration with others in your team or organisation may be useful. Consider putting together a resources file with anonymised sample letters, forms, etc., that could be used by students and other learners. Incorporate a range of styles and approaches to enable the learner to understand that different approaches are acceptable (when this is the case).

Feedback from service users

It is now widely accepted that feedback from service users and carers is an essential component of the assessment of learners' practice in health and social care (Levin, 2004; GSCC, 2005). The main reason their role in assessment is considered to be so important is because they can provide insight into assessment judgements that could not be achieved by other people (Hastings, 2000).

Practice educators should be working to involve service users and carers in both learning and assessment within a wide range of learning and professional development activities. It is all too easy for this aspect of work-based education to be an 'add-on' but, if genuine partnership with service users is to be achieved, their voice must be heard in all aspects of service provision, including the training and education of professionals (Levin, 2004). However, although the importance of involving users and carers in part or all of an assessment is recognised, there are a number of difficulties and many of the methods used are still being evaluated. One of the key issues is the avoidance of serious bias. People who have received a service may have their opinions shaped by the outcomes of the learner's work with them (which could be outside of the learner's control) rather than the learner's actual competence. They may also be influenced by how much they liked the learner, wanting to help the learners they liked with a good assessment and penalise those who they didn't like with a poor assessment. Fairness can also be an issue because service users may not fully understand the criteria for measuring success and they may find benchmarking very difficult, particularly when their experience of social workers is fairly limited (expectations may be too high or too low). Furthermore, it is not usually possible to engage with every service user and selecting a limited number to represent the whole user group can be problematic – it is impossible to know if the views of the selected few are representative of the whole group.

One of the real dangers of including feedback from service users and carers in assessment is that their involvement can be tokenistic. However, many believe that with adequate support, training and preparation it is possible for them to make valuable and meaningful contributions to the whole educational process (e.g. Levin, 2004). However, the majority of feedback on learners' performance is still most commonly gathered through questionnaires sent out to selected service users; for example, by qualifying social work students (Moriarty, et al., 2010). At this level there really is a danger that seeking feedback becomes a token gesture. Careful thought needs to be given to ensuring that service users approached in this way are empowered to make meaningful and valid contributions.

ACTIVITY 11.7

Design a brief questionnaire to send out to users of your service to obtain feedback on one very specific aspect of a learner's practice.

Comment

Think how you could empower service users to make a meaningful contribution by providing information that would help them to understand what was expected from them, together with guidance on the criteria for the assessment. Remember to keep all guidance simple, straightforward and easy to understand.

Because feedback from service users will be an important tool, not just for assessment but also for learning, learners should be involved in deciding how and when service users are approached and should be fully informed of any responses received.

REFLECTION POINT

Hastings (2000) suggests that social work learners should have 'user supervisors' to work with them throughout their education to help gain insight into the user perspective. These supervisors would also be involved in assessing the learner – what do you think? Could this work in your workplace?

Could the principle be extended to qualified experienced social workers to help with their continuing professional development?

Feedback from colleagues/other professionals

The final method we will consider is feedback from colleagues and other professionals. As with feedback from service users and carers, this is a valuable source of information and can provide insight and other perspectives on a learner's practice. However, it is worth bearing in mind that experienced professionals do not necessarily have the skills or knowledge to contribute meaningfully and fairly to the assessment of learners. Crisp, et al. (2006) point out that willingness to participate in the process of assessment does not guarantee competence as an assessor. Anyone who is asked to provide feedback that will contribute to the assessment of a learner should be made aware of the learner's intended learning outcomes and must fully understand the assessment criteria that they should use.

It is a good idea to ask colleagues/other professionals to make a specific contribution to assessment rather than a general one; for example, to comment on a specific competence or to undertake an observation of practice with negotiated assessment objectives. Some information, training and support may be needed to enable colleagues to participate in this way.

Summary of Part Three Domain C

- Making assessment strategies and methods, and the criteria used to assess them, clear and transparent is essential for the learner to progress.
- Getting the assessment 'wrong', i.e. misaligning it with the rest of the learning scheme, is likely to block learning and inhibit performance.
- While it is important for the safety of service users that social workers' competence to practise is directly assessed in practice, it is also important to use assessment techniques that enable work-based assessors to gain an insight into the learner's transferable skills, such as the ability to construct and reconstruct knowledge and to think critically, because these are essential components of the broader professional capability.
- When designing an assessment strategy it is important to understand what you are aiming to achieve through the assessment process.
- 'Good' assessment is:
  - relevant;
  - valid;
  - reliable;
  - sufficient;
  - authentic.
- Assessing professional capability in the workplace requires a flexible and creative approach.
- Assessment methods. The tool that you choose should:
  - aligned with your intended learning outcome;
  - relevant, valid, reliable, sufficient and authentic;
  - take into account your work environment, service users and the learner.
- To overcome some of the difficulties with assessment, practice educators can triangulate pieces of evidence.
- The nature of the assessment task that you will be facing is complex and highly dependent on the local circumstances of the learning experience you have provided.

FURTHER READING

Levin, E (2004) *Resource Guide 2: Involving service users and carers in social work education*. SCIE, available at **www.scie.org.uk/publications/resource guides/rg02/index.asp**
This is a very useful resource providing ideas for involving service users and carers in social work education.

Social Work Education (2006), 25 (4).
This is a special edition of this journal which explores and critically evaluates the involvement of users and carers in social work education. It contains papers written from professional, educational and service-user perspectives.

Davies, H and Kinloch, H (2000) Critical incident analysis: Facilitating reflection and transfer of learning. In Cree, V E and Macauley, C (eds) *Transfer of learning in professional and vocational education*. London and New York: Routledge.
Provides a very good exploration of the use of critical incident analysis.

Part Four
Domain D: Effective continuing performance as a practice educator

Meeting the requirements of the Practice Educator Professional Standards (CSW, 2012)

The material in this part links to the following domain standards.

Domain D: Effective continuing performance as a practice educator

Practice educators at Stage 2 should:

1. Critically reflect upon and evaluate own professional development and apply learning to subsequent practice education experience using a range of methods.

2. Demonstrate critical reflection on own development as practice educator including the use of feedback from direct observations, colleagues and HEI tutors and other assessment sources.

3. Demonstrate knowledge of current HEI quality assurance systems and ability to liaise and negotiate HEI processes.

4. Maintain information and data relevant to the development of practice.

5. Demonstrate an applied knowledge of contemporary issues in research, policy, legislation and practice including agency policy, procedures and practice.

6. Demonstrate an ability to transfer practice educator skills and knowledge to new roles in mentoring, supervision, teaching and/or assessment.

Introduction to Domain D

As seen throughout this book, before we can enable others we need to enable ourselves. As a practice educator you need to feel confident not only in your ability to facilitate the development of transferable skills in others but also in your ability to develop these skills within your own practice. You should be applying the methods and standards you are advocating to yourself first, in order to model the processes and develop your own understanding of them. Understanding your views of knowing and learning, your approach to learning, your learning style preferences, and developing a reflective competency all become the basis of lifelong learning for practice educators. Part Two explored a number of these views, approaches and preferences and showed how they can affect the way you enable and facilitate others and therefore impact on your potential achievement as a practice educator.

Part Four now develops these and other ideas further in our final chapter to enable you to create an individual approach for effective continuing practice and fulfil the requirements of Domain D. This part of the book may be shorter than the others and concentrated in just one chapter, but its ideas are the foundation upon which good practice is established and sustained.

Chapter 12
Continuing learning and development

Critically understanding yourself as a learner

As Lefevre (2005) argues, creating supportive, safe and trusting environments in which learning is facilitated and risks can be taken requires enhanced self-reflection and self-awareness to ensure you are sufficiently conscious of the impact of your behaviour on the learner, and can realistically evaluate the nature of the environment you are co-creating.

ACTIVITY 12.1

Using the material from Chapter 5 write an insightful profile of yourself as a learner (e.g. on the practice educator programme). Using this profile, note the aspect that appears to influence your learning the most. How can being more aware of this help enable:
(a) your own learning?
(b) the learning of others?
(c) anyone enabling you; for example, your mentor?

Comment

Understanding yourself as a learner can unlock further potential. The key is to find ways to maximise the good aspects and minimise the bad ones, and these may differ in respect of whom you are interacting with and the nature of your role with them. For example, being an active learner may mean that you have high levels of motivation – you can make the most of this by allowing yourself the necessary time to put your ideas into action properly. On the other hand, a mentor or supervisor may ask you to take time to stop and think as well, and you will need to remember to check to see whether your active enthusiasm is overwhelming less confident learners.

Professional learning and development

A holistic approach

A recent review (Webster-Wright, 2009) of professional development has advocated a 'continuing professional learning' (CPL) approach, focusing on professionals being engaged holistically in self-directed, ongoing learning. This approach avoids the potential limitations of the phrase 'professional development', which can view professional practitioners as deficient and in need of development through enforced training, which remains at a surface level. The

CPL approach sees the learner, the context and the learning as interrelated, and therefore the learning is deeper and more personal.

Whatever terminology is applied, though, the development of your own practice can only become more meaningful when experiential (informal) as well as more formal learning activities are planned and engaged with in such a way that they enable significant, relevant insights and new understandings to emerge. Recognising the need to make the most of informal as well as more formal learning should become a natural feature of practice. Informal learning covers areas like observation, feedback, dialogue, and co-working, and usually results in new knowing or understanding that is either tacit or regarded as part of a person's general capability, rather than as something 'learned'. Nevertheless, it is a key area for professional development. For example, Becher (1999) reports that professionals learn six times as much through non-formal as through formal means.

Independent, self-directed learning

It is, therefore, practitioners who have the skills, abilities and attributes of self-directed and reflective learners who should be able to make the most of the potential for learning found within all work situations (Brown and Rutter, 2008). However, the ever-present danger, as with any skill set, is that it becomes routine and unexamined. Here, again, an embedded, holistic and critical stance can help to foster a more critical engagement, which will lead to deeper and more meaningful self-directed and ongoing learning.

We can look at this in more detail by listing the skills and abilities of self-directed, reflective learners and adding to each of them the extra element that a critical approach brings.

- Take the initiative in diagnosing your learning needs – a critical approach also asks:
  - What type of information informs this diagnosis – feedback, evaluation, meetings, learner reactions, gut feeling...?
  - Who provides the input and how – colleagues, supervisors, managers, learners...?
  - How honest and/or informed am I about my areas of strength and weakness?
  - What prompts me to take action, and what stops me?
- Recognise and capture the learning potential of everyday events – a critical approach also asks:
  - How and when do I note colleagues' ideas, tips, methods of working as useful or as areas of need within my own working practices?
  - If a learner is not performing well, how do I analyse my part of the responsibility?
- Critically reflect on your practice and its outcomes – a critical approach also asks:
  - Who critically questions me?
  - Have I actively sought a direct observation of my practice?
  - Did/do I record my reflection and use it for the practice educator programme?
  - Do I ensure my reflection is strengths-based as well?
- Create your own learning objectives – a critical approach also asks:
  - How do I use any input or diagnosis to form an objective for myself?
  - Do I discuss it with anyone?
- Identify, locate and evaluate the resources needed – a critical approach also asks:
  - What happens if the resources are not there?
  - Who else could help me?

- Choose and implement appropriate learning strategies – a critical approach also asks:
  - Do I review a full range of styles and approaches as well as my particular preferences?
  - How do I ensure that new knowledge, skills or ideas are put into practice and not left as a collection of notes or handouts?
  - How do I try to overcome the negativity associated with an organisation or team culture that is not conducive to learning?

- Evaluate learning outcomes – a critical approach also asks:
  - Do I revisit my learning objectives?
  - Do I test whether my practice has changed and how?
  - Do I actively seek and reflect on more critical feedback from learners or colleagues in order to gain a different perspective?
  - Do I reflect on feedback from assessed work undertaken within the practice educator programme or other programmes?
  - No one can be expected to practise perfectly – how do I judge whether my aims and expectations are set too high?

- Digest and generalise learning in order to facilitate its transfer – a critical approach also asks:
  - When I reflect on the learning gained from a specific situation, do I start to articulate it in more general ideas and concepts? For example, *I want to use the reflective question my supervisor used on me with other students – it was such an effective deep-learning prompt. . .*
  - Do I connect this to learning theories or research findings I have used or seen? How do I make connections between different areas of learning and different situations looking for common elements (e.g. across supervision, mentoring or coaching situations); or for different types of learners?

As we can see, it is not enough to have experiences and passively expect to learn from them. It is important that you take an active approach to learning and practice, and engage in all aspects of planning, undertaking, monitoring, reflecting on and evaluating your learning (Jarvis, 1992), bringing experiential and critically reflective processes together.

Stress and emotions

However, the more emotional and personal elements of learning must also be appreciated. We know that elements such as anxiety, fear, and demotivation become barriers to learning, but so do more mundane but fundamental issues such as lack of time, support and resources for learning. Indeed, there seem to be much less time, opportunity or support for deep reflective thinking at work (Clutterbuck, 2001). On top of this, excessive work pressures and managerialist cultures create feelings of helplessness, anxiety and of being out of control, which all conspire against reflective practice. This is the reality of practice today for many people, and so a key part of being a professional is the need to find your own approach for dealing with it as best you can (i.e. to minimise the adverse effects on yourself, your colleagues and your service users). Thompson and Thompson (2008, p135) show that the busier we are, the more reflective we need to be in order to think more clearly and carefully before we act – *if the pressure to get things done means that we do not have time to think about what we are doing, then the potential for things to go wrong is high*, and that could waste a lot more precious time.

Of course, we are only human and there are times when the strategies we use to cope can be instinctive but not the most appropriate for long-term survival. Berne's (1996) work looking at 'the games people play' still appears very relevant in helping explain what happens to us. I'm sure we all know people who go into 'controlling parent' or 'disruptive child' mode when the pressure is on, and I'm sure we must all have gone down the 'ain't it awful' route, moaning about how bad things are but then actually wallowing in it as everyone joins in. It is always worthwhile revisiting this book and others like it to help become more aware of and re-evaluate our behaviour and coping mechanisms, and re-establish a more 'adult' approach where necessary.

On a personal note, when trying to write this book we have both felt deep levels of stress, frustration and anxiety, and resorted to avoidance, denial, and a range of displacement activities as the pressure mounted. However, what we both found was that once we made a decision to not let the pressure get to us or 'go under', we were more able to reassert ourselves and find a few solutions (e.g. renegotiating deadlines) that helped us to manage the situation more effectively. The feeling of being overwhelmed seemed to not only demotivate us but also disempower us, and this was the pivotal issue we needed to address first.

ACTIVITY **12.2**

What can you do to avoid the spiral of helplessness and demoralisation that results from excessive pressure of work and time constraints?

Comment

Noting that this is actually happening is the first step and making a concerted effort to manage it as best you can is the next – maintaining self-awareness as well as retaining some measure of control are key starting points. Forcing yourself to stop and think, even if it is only for a few minutes, brings that element of control back into the process. Thompson and Thompson (2008) also stress the importance of not losing sight of what you are doing and why, and being aware of your own role in the process too. They provide useful discussion around minimising the impact of other barriers such as lack of organisational commitment or value placed on reflective practice, which may be helpful to you.

Critically informed practice

Keeping up to date

Critically informed practice involves keeping up to date with the world of practice education, i.e. finding out about new knowledge, processes, ideas and policies, etc., from a wide range of individuals, groups and organisations. It also means keeping in touch with learning and training developers within your organisation and the learning providers within your area, finding out what is on offer and supporting their work.

ACTIVITY 12.3

Research a range of local and national groups associated with social work practice education. Note the types of information, advice and help available from each.

Comment

There will be local learning resource networks (LRNs) to be aware of, as well as some key national organisations, such as:

- Social Care Institute for Excellence (SCIE – www.scie.org.uk);
- National Organisation for Practice Teaching (England) (NOPT – www.nopt.org);
- Skills for Care (SfC – www.skillsforcare.org.uk);
- Children's Workforce Development Council (CWDC – www.cwdcouncil.org.uk);
- Scottish Social Services Learning Network (www.learningnetworks.org.uk);
- Scottish Organisation for Practice Teaching (ScOPT – www.scopt.co.uk);
- Making Practice-Based Learning Work (www.practicebasedlearning.org).

After you have finished your practice education programme, many university resources may no longer be available to you. In this respect, several of the national sources outlined above, as well as your local and agency resources, may be useful to locate relevant theory, research, legislation, policy and quality-assurance guidance.

Linking knowledge, knowing and action

In order to link knowledge, knowing and action, a slightly different emphasis needs to be applied to the more traditional notions of theory–practice integration and to evidence-based practice (while still adhering to the essence of accountable and informed practice). We need to open up these notions and allow a more critical and holistic approach to the use of knowledge within your practice as an educator.

We have seen that students and novice practitioners may want more direction and 'rules' to follow and will look to more formal, external knowledge to provide it, as their range of experiential knowledge and more tacit knowing will be limited. Similarly, in your early days as a practice educator you will be looking for 'external' answers that can help you (e.g. from books or journals). You will not want to let your learner down any more than you would a service user. However, you will also be drawing on your existing knowledge and tacit under-standing (e.g. about interacting and working with people), asking advice from others, and building up a bank of experience and expertise in the process.

To demonstrate this we can work through an example using yourself and Liz, a second-year student. Liz does not seem motivated in her placement with you, she is not engaged with the service users and appears uninterested in learning. You want to find out more in order to help you decide what to do and your questions will reflect this. (The following section is adapted from work by Ashford and Lecroy, 1991.)

If you start with the practice situation then your tactical questions will be situational and specific:

- *How can I motivate Liz?*

You may struggle to answer this question on your own if this is your first experience with a student. You may know that this is not Liz's first choice of placement and obviously suspect this is a major part of the problem.

More strategic questions would prompt you to seek other people's ideas to help:

- *What do other practice educators do to motivate students on placement?*

- *What does Liz's university tutor know about this?*

Using these types of questions you can gain more information from different perspectives about the situation, and also a range of ideas that helped in different situations but which may be applicable here. Liz's tutor may tell you more about her specific learning needs. A practice teacher who works near you may say that in her experience, demotivated learners are always hiding something and it is always worth 'digging' further. A report on the SCIE website may note how students get very blinkered about meeting particular professional requirements on placement.

Knowledge-seeking questions allow a wider perspective on the problem and more general understandings which help you to construct your answer:

- *What is learner motivation?*

- *Which factors are likely to increase learner motivation?*

The 'answers' found using more formal sources (e.g. books and journals) will be general and perhaps vague but they may provide additional insight into the problem. You might read up more on theories about motivation – extrinsic/intrinsic, or revisit Maslow's (1943) theory of human motivation and 'hierarchy of needs' model.

All these ideas can be evaluated in their own right and then related to the situation and appraised against what you know about Liz and the learning context to see how relevant they are and how they might help. For example, you may then decide that you respect the practice teacher and trust her advice, that the tutor has highlighted an issue about the PCF that Liz didn't mention, and you can see that motivation theory highlights the link between anxiety and motivation and this resonates with other behaviour you've noticed in Liz. You may decide to revisit the learning contract with Liz and critically question her understanding of her own needs. You may see that Liz is really worried that the type of work she is doing is not relating to the professional standards she needs to address this year – it is her fear that is the demotivating factor. By more fully addressing the links between the work and the PCF successfully, Liz becomes much more motivated.

There are three key points to reiterate here. First, the type of 'evidence' you use in practice can include informal as well as formal types and sources (Humphries, 2003; Trevithick, 2007), i.e. knowing as well as knowledge. Other people's ideas, reflective output, experiential learning, feedback and values should have a key place alongside more formal types of knowledge such as theory, research, policy and quality guidelines. Second, knowledge and knowing can be used in a number of ways. They can help at all stages of problem forming and solving, rather than just be applied mechanistically to provide an 'answer'. This helps ensure that the best understanding of a situation is created at the outset, which, in turn, informs aims, choices, decisions and outcomes, as illustrated in the process below.

- What is going on – name and frame the situation. Knowledge and knowing provide awareness, description, explanation, and understanding of wider, specific and underlying (assumptions, givens) or hidden issues (ethical, moral), etc.

- What is needed – establish purpose/develop feasible aims and objectives. Knowledge and knowing provide ideas, directions, possibilities, alternatives, etc.

- What to do about it – consider alternatives. Knowledge and knowing provide general approaches and strategies as well as specific techniques and methods for consideration, etc.

- Make a decision. Knowledge and knowing provide further direction and detail on chosen approaches, strategies and methods, etc.

- Noting what might happen – take account of impact and outcomes with monitoring and review stages. Knowledge and knowing provide awareness of possible effects, implications, dangers, results, etc.

The third and final point concerns evaluation. All types of knowledge and knowing need to be evaluated in respect of authority, reliability, credibility and accessibility, and, of course, relevance and ability to understand the situation and answer your questions. The criteria used need to be appropriate to the source. Obviously, you cannot judge the applicability of a piece of research in the same way as a theoretical model or reflective learning outcomes. A range of criteria for critical appraisal of arguments, research and theory can be found in Brown and Rutter (2008, pp11–12).

ACTIVITY 12.4

Which criteria do you use to evaluate someone else's ideas gained from their experience and learning?

Comment

The range of criteria which may be useful probably relate to the idea of 'authority' or 'expertise' – does this person know their 'stuff' (e.g. judging the type and range of experience this person has had which may affect their reliability and credibility)? Other aspects may relate more to the type of person they are and the approach they take to others (e.g. their values, self-awareness, the way they talk and listen to others, especially those less experienced or less 'powerful'). How we view the opinions of others can also take a less critical path by unconsciously valuing only those who look, talk, or act like us, or whom we like. We sometimes need to consciously reappraise these opinions and our view of them.

By using a range of knowledge and knowing, and allowing it to inform practice through a set of critical review and thinking processes, the 'best' outcome is more likely to be achieved. The overall point to be made is that good practice is an ongoing process of information-gathering and evaluation – knowledge and knowing need to be kept up to date and evaluated, as well as made meaningful to the situations you are working in.

Critically reflective practice – knowing, acting and being

Reflection – a review

We know that critically reflective practitioners are self-aware, critically analysing, evaluating, reviewing and updating their values, skills and knowledge, practising flexibly and reflexively, exploring alternative approaches and being open to change in all contexts – not just those concerned with learning. They are, in effect, demonstrating professional capability and criticality in all aspects of Barnett and Coate's (2005) model (knowing, acting and being). This means that ongoing learning and development are not just about updating knowledge and skills, they are also about reconsidering your ability to make sound judgements and decisions. They involve engagement with, and reflection on experience, which facilitates the promotion of professional values and principles which guide action (Tyreman, 2000, p122).

As we have seen, reflection should be:

- active – lead to active output or change;
- holistic and meaningful – integrate knowing, acting and being;
- developmental – explicit to implicit areas of practice, recognise and develop own methods;
- critical – evaluating competence and capability; looking at strengths and weaknesses;
- deep – any frameworks being used need to encompass critical levels of description, analysis and evaluation;
- enhanced by dialogue and critical questioning with others.

A humble stance

However, even more than this, reflection is about embodying the nature and values of a profession – i.e. when you become a social work practice educator, rather than just knowing something about it or going through the motions of doing it. However, although many competency-type skills may be easily reflected on and self-appraised, your disposition at work and the approaches you take to work situations will be so closely tied in with your personality and previous history that a truly honest reflective examination can be very difficult to achieve. As we know, reflection can become very negative unless it is also strengths-based, but it can also become self-justifying and self-serving – 'I reflect, therefore I am ok!'

The need for humility as well as honesty within a reflective stance is perhaps a key point here. It especially holds true when you are working in a partnership of trust with a learner. You have to model reflective behaviour in order to be credible but the extra awareness that humility can bring to the process may help address some of the power issues between educators and learners; it may enhance sensitivity towards the learner's perspective.

CASE STUDY 12.1

Carol had critically thought through how she could help Vik to manage his learning more productively. She thought Vik was a great student but quite disorganised in his approach. Carol thought that Vik needed a system and as she didn't want to impose her

continued

CASE STUDY 12.1 *continued*

own, she spoke to him about the need for a more systematic approach and provided him with a range of ideas he could adopt. From Carol's point of view she thought she had helped him. However, Vik thought about it very differently – in his mind Carol was now criticising him and it made him doubt himself. He knew he was a little disorganised but it hadn't affected his work in any significant way. In fact, Carol had praised his work in the past but now he doubted whether she had meant it. He became hypercritical about everything he was doing and the anxiety this provoked made him start to resent Carol. In their meetings Vik became unresponsive. Carol sought his opinion but Vik didn't feel confident or safe enough to give it. The relationship began to deteriorate. Carol noticed this and reflected with a trusted colleague about it. Gradually it dawned on her that whatever she had thought of Vik's disorganised way, this was only her view of the situation. She had judged it as 'wrong' and something that needed to be changed, but in the bigger picture, even though he was a bit disorganised, it didn't really matter – Vik was still a great student. By imposing her own interpretation on the matter, no matter how well thought through it had been, she had effectively 'oppressed' Vik, and this had undermined his confidence and motivation. In their next meeting Carol made an unconditional apology and discussed how her need to be in control of the placement had blinded her to the fact that it was two-person responsibility. She admitted she was worried about Vik's disorganised methods but she should have talked about this first with him to establish together, in partnership, whether they were an issue or not, rather than judging the situation alone and trying to take control.

Just as it does for your learners, developing practice in this way can prove threatening and provoke anxiety for you. It is hard work, involving self-doubt and mental blocks, and therefore needs to be supported and enabled in empowering work-based relationships and partnerships, i.e. genuine learning cultures. Some of you may be fortunate enough to work in a positive learning culture that encourages sharing of knowledge, plus feedback and evaluation of services; others of you may need to seek such a relationship more actively; for example, on a one-to-one mentoring basis with a colleague you trust.

REFLECTION POINT

Where are your risk-free, safe opportunities for:
- *emotional support?*
- *discussing different perspectives?*
- *critical questioning and challenge?*
- *exploring alternative approaches, ideas, outcomes?*
- *fully exploring how you deal with complexity, risk, uncertainty?*
- *making new theory–practice connections?*
- *feedback?*

As we noted at the start of this chapter, an ongoing approach to professional development sees the learner, the context and the learning as interrelated, and therefore the whole experience is deeper and more personal for you. This approach not only requires your commitment and dedication, it also requires recognition, value, encouragement, and support from others around you.

Summary of Part Four Domain D

- You need to feel confident not only in your ability to facilitate the development of transferable skills but also in your ability to model their use within your own practice.
- Critical engagement will lead to deeper and more meaningful self-directed and ongoing learning.
- Part of being a professional is the need to find your own approach for dealing with stress – maintaining self-awareness while retaining some measure of control are key starting points.
- Good practice is an ongoing process of information-gathering and evaluation – knowledge and knowing need to be kept up to date and evaluated, as well as made meaningful to the situations you are working in.
- There is a need for humility as well as honesty within a reflective stance to ensure the best type of partnership can be established with your learners.

FURTHER READING

Brown, K and Rutter, L (2008) *Critical thinking for social work*. 2nd edition. Exeter: Learning Matters.

A pragmatic look at some ideas associated with critical thinking, especially those linked to learning and development.

Fook, J and Gardner, F (2007) *Practising critical reflection: A handbook*. Maidenhead: Open University Press.

This very accessible book takes a theoretical and a practical approach, offering skills, strategies and tools.

Rolfe, G, Freshwater, D and Jasper, M (2001) *Critical reflection for the nursing and helping professions. A user's guide*. London: Palgrave.

This practical user's guide offers a range of clear frameworks and structures for reflective practice, including individual and group supervision, reflective writing and reflective research.

Thompson, S and Thompson, N (2008) *The critically reflective practitioner*. Basingstoke: Palgrave Macmillan.

This is essential reading for making sense of reflective practice, looking at what it is not and what it can be at its best.

Conclusion

So, what effects will work-based learning and critical reflection have on qualifying practitioners and established staff? What should the enabling and facilitation of learning be achieving? How will practitioners be developing? If you refer back to the Barnett and Coate (2005) theory of professional capability, by following a creative approach to the enabling of learning and professional development you should be facilitating practitioners to work and learn independently, to deal with complexity and embrace change, i.e. develop and enhance critical practice.

As we have seen, critical practice is constructive, creative and optimistic, and takes calculated risks as part of a positive strategy of addressing issues and problems rather than avoiding them (Adams et al., 2002, p94). It is worth repeating, though, that critical practice is not about 'being certain', but about being able to deal with uncertainty using sound, valid and accountable processes and, where appropriate, maintain a position of 'respectful uncertainty', or at least hold onto doubt for longer and seek out other possible versions (Taylor and White, 2006). Critical practice therefore deals creatively with uncertainty and complexity rather than following prescriptions, and is capable of change. As Fook, et al. (2000) also show, developing professional expertise is a process of learning to work with uncertainty using a wide range of knowledge, skills and understanding. When developing expertise, professionals start to create their own 'theories' of practice – their constructed knowledge about the best way to do things.

By developing your learners to approach their learning in active and critically reflective ways, and by using student-centred, active and critically reflective methods yourself, the learning situations you create will better enable such techniques and attributes of critical practice and expertise to develop or become enhanced. In addition, the best type of work-based learning can help all participants to see their processes of reasoning and judgement more realistically and to become more reflexive, analytical and systematic in their 'sense-making' activities (Taylor and White, 2006, p950). So, we may all learn from this involvement in learning as the relative importance of learning from experience becomes greater the more expert we become. Many of our students are amazed at how much they learned about themselves and their own practice while undertaking an enabling role. Indeed, one of the points to emphasise here is that the development of professional capability and expertise is a complex form of growth, which is never complete. The journey begins at the pre-qualification stage of a professional's career but will be a lifelong learning task, and so your part in another's development will be just that – a part, and in your own life it will form just another strand within the growth of your expertise.

Perhaps this is a way to build true communities of practice which reject the separation of training and learning from practice (Lave and Wenger, 1991) and enable the organisation to learn as well through more pervasive and distributed routes (Gould, 2000). This is what makes the role of the practice educator so crucial to the enabling of learning organisations and is why the College of Social Work has introduced the Practice Educator Professional Standards.

Overall, enabling learning requires innovation, courage and the willingness to try new methods and experiment. Enthusiasm and adaptability are key factors. However, it can also create its own set of anxieties, especially when new skills are being developed. As with any type of activity, much is learned through trial and error to see what will best fit your particular situation. 'Mistakes' help create a bank of expertise, so don't worry too much when things don't go to plan. It is important to review the learning schemes you design, involve the learner in a true partnership, evaluate how well you are doing, be flexible, and adapt and change where necessary. Being enthusiastic about your work and caring about the learners you are working with are the main attributes they require from you.

We hope this book has helped you to understand yourself as an enabler and to form your ideas about what good practice should entail; finally, we wish you the very best in all your future 'enabling' endeavours.

References

Adams, R, Dominelli, L and Payne, M (eds) (2002) *Critical practice in social work*. London: Palgrave.

Anderson, L W and Krathwohl, D R (eds) (2001) *A taxonomy for learning, teaching, and assessing: A revision of Bloom's taxonomy of educational objectives*. New York: Longman.

Argyris, C and Schön, D A (1974) *Theory in practice. Increasing professional effectiveness*. San Francisco: Jossey-Bass Publishers.

Argyris, C and Schön, D A (1978) *Organisational learning:A theory of action perpsective*. Reading, Mass.: Addison Wesley.

Ashford, J B and Lecroy, C W (1991) Problem solving in social work practice: Implications for knowledge utilisation. *Research in Social Work Practice*, 1, 306–18.

Atherton, J S (2009a) *Learning and teaching; Advance organisers*. **www.doceo.co.uk/l&t/teaching/advance_organisers.htm**

Atherton, J S (2009b) *Learning and teaching: Learning curves*. **www.learningandteaching.info/learning/learning_curve.htm**

Bandura, A (1977) *Social learning theory*. New York: General Learning Press.

Barnett, R (1997) *Higher education: A critical business*. Buckingham: Society for Research in Higher Education and Open University Press.

Barnett, R and Coate, K (2005) *Engaging the curriculum in higher education*. Maidenhead: Open University Press.

Baume, D (2004) *Reflective competence*. **www.businessballs.com/consciouscompetence learningmodel.htm**

Baxter Magolda, M (1996) Epistemological development in graduate and professional education. *Review of Higher Education*, 19 (3), 283–304.

Becher, T (1999) Quality in the professions. *Studies in Higher Education,* 19 (2), 225–35.

Beddoe, L (2009) Creating continuous conversation: Social workers and learning organizations. *Social Work Education – The International Journal*, 28(7), 722–36.

Berne, E (1996) *Games people play*. New York: Ballantine Books.

Beverley, A and Worsley, A (2007) *Learning and teaching in social work practice*. London: Palgrave Macmillan.

Biggs, J (1999) What the student does: Teaching for enhanced learning. *Higher Education Research and Development*,18 (1), 57–75.

Biggs, J (2003) *Teaching for quality learning at university*, 2nd edition. Buckingham: SRHE and Open University Press.

Bloom, B S (ed.) (1956) *Taxonomy of educational objectives, the classification of educational goals – Handbook I: cognitive domain*. New York: McKay.

Boud, D (1999) Avoiding the traps: Seeking good practice in the use of self assessment and reflection on professional course. *Social Work Education*, 18, 121–31.

Boud, D, Cressey, P and Docherty, P (eds) (2006) *Productive reflection at work*. Abingdon: Routledge.

Boud, D, Keogh, R and Walker, D (1985) *Reflection: Turning experience into learning*. London: Croom Helm.

Bowlby, D (1969) *Attachment and loss: vol 1, attachment*. New York: Basic Books.

Brockbank, A and McGill, I (2002) *Facilitating reflective learning through mentoring and coaching*. London: Kogan Page.

Brookfield, S (1987) *Developing critical thinkers*. Milton Keynes: Open University Press.

Brown, G (2001) *Assessment: A guide for lecturers*. Assessment Series No 3. London: The Higher Education Academy. **www.heacademy.ac.uk**

Brown, K, Fenge, L and Young, N (2005) Researching reflective practice: An example from post qualifying social work education. *Research in Post Compulsory Education,* (10) 3, 389–402.

Brown K, Keen, S, Rutter, L and Warren, A (2010) *Partnerships, CPD & APL: Supporting workforce development across the social care sector*. Birmingham: Learn to Care.

Brown, K and Rutter, L (2008) *Critical thinking in social work*. 2nd edition. Exeter: Learning Matters.

Bruner, J (1960) *The process of education*. Cambridge, Mass.: Harvard University Press.

Cartney, P (2000) Adult learning styles: Implications for practice teaching in social work. *Social Work Education*, 19 (6), 609–26.

CCETSW (1995) *Assuring quality in the diploma in social sork – Rules and requirements for the DIPSW*. London: CCETSW.

Chapman, A (c.2009) *Conscious competence learning mode*. **www.businessballs.com/cons ciouscompetencelearningmodel.htm**

Cherry, N (2005) Preparing for practice in the age of complexity. *Higher Education Research and Development*, 24 (4), 309–20.

Clapton, G, Cree, V, Allan, M, Edwards, R, Forbes, R, Irwin, M, Paterson, W and Perry, R (2006) Grasping the nettle: Integrating learning and practice revisited and reimagined. *Social Work Education*, 25 (6), 645–56.

Clutterbuck, D (2001) *Everyone needs a mentor. Fostering talent at work*. 3rd edition. London: Chartered Institute of Personnel and Development.

Coffield, F, Moseley, D, Hall, E and Ecclestone, K (2004) *Learning styles and pedagogy in post-16 learning: A systematic and critical review*. London: Learning Skills Research Centre (now LSN).

Collingwood, P (2005) The three stage theory framework. Building an Identikit picture. *The Journal of Practice Teaching*, 6 (1), 6–23.

Collingwood, P, Emond, R and Woodward, R (2008) The theory circle: A tool for learning and for practice. *Social Work Education*, 27 (1), 70–83.

Cooper, B (2008) Continuing professional development: A critical approach. In Fraser, S and Matthews, S (eds) *The critical practitioner in social work and health care*. London: Sage, 222–37.

Cowburn, M, Nelson, P and Williams, J (2000) Assessment of social work students: Standpoint and strong objectivity. *Social Work Education*, 19 (6), 627–37.

Cree, V (2000) The challenge of assessment. In Cree, V and Macauley, C (eds) *Transfer of learning in professional and vocational education*. London: Routledge, 27–52.

Cree V E, Macaulay, C and Loney, H (1998) *Transfer of learning: A study*. Edinburgh: CCETSW and Scottish Office Central Research Unit.

Crisp, B, Green Lister, P and Dutton, K (2006) Not just social work academics: The involvement of others in the assessment of social work students. *Social Work Education*, 25 (7), 723–34.

CSW (2012) www.collegeofsocialwork.org

Davies, H and Kinloch, H (2000) Critical incident analysis: Facilitating reflection and transfer of learning. In Cree, V and Macauley, C (eds) *Transfer of learning in professional and vocational education*. London: Routledge, 137–47.

Davys, A M and Beddoe, L (2009) The reflective learning model: Supervision of social work students. *Social Work Education*, 28 (8), 919–33.

Disability Discrimination Act (1995) www.opsi.gov.uk

Doel, M (2010) *Social work placement. A traveller's guide*. Abingdon: Routledge.

Doel, M and Shardlow, S (1998) *The new social work practice: Exercises and activities for training and developing social workers*. Aldershot: Arena.

Doel, M, Sawdon, C and Morrison, D (2002) *Learning, practice and assessment*. London: Jessica Kingsley.

Doel, M, Shardlow, S, Sawdon, C and Sawdon, D (1996) *Teaching social work practice*. Aldershot: Arena.

DoH (2002) *Requirements for social work training*. London: Department of Health.

Entwistle, N and Ramsden, P (1983) *Understanding student learning*. London: Croom Helm.

Eraut, M (1994) *Developing professional knowledge and competence*. London: Falmer.

Eraut, M, Alderton, J and Cole, G (1998) *Development of knowledge and skills in employment*. Brighton: University of Sussex.

Fook, J and Gardner, F (2007) *Practising critical reflection. A resource handbook*. Maidenhead: Open University Press.

Fook, J, Ryan, M and Hawkins, L (2000) *Professional expertise: Practice, theory and education for working in uncertainty*. London: Whiting and Birch Ltd.

Ford, K and Jones, A (1987) *Student supervision*. BASW Practical Social Work series. London: Macmillan.

Ford, P, Johnston, B, Mitchell, R, Brumfit, C and Myles, F (2005) Practice learning and the development of students as critical practitioners – some findings from research. *Social Work Education,* 24 (4), 391–407.

Fraser, S, and Matthews, S (2008) *The critical practitioner in social work and health care.* London: Sage.

Furness, S and Gilligan, P (2004) Fitness for purpose: Issues from practice placements, practice teaching and the assessment of student practice. *Social Work Education,* 23 (4), 465–79.

Gardner, H (1993) *Frames of mind: The theory of multiple intelligences.* 2nd edition. New York: Basic Books.

Gould, N (2000) Becoming a learning organisation: A social work example. *Social Work Education,* 19 (6), 585–96.

Gould, N and Baldwin, M (eds) (2004) *Social work, critical reflection and the learning organisation.* Aldershot: Ashgate.

Grey, D (2002) *A briefing on work-based learning.* Generic Centre Assessment Series No.11. London: Higher Education Academy.

GSCC (2002) *Guidance on the assessment of practice in the workplace.* London: General Social Care Council. **www.gscc.org.uk**

GSCC (2005) *The revised post qualification framework for social work education and training.* London: General Social Care Council. **www.gscc.org.uk**

GSCC (2006) *Specialist standards and requirements for post-qualifying social work education and training. Practice education.* London: General Social Care Council. **www.gscc.org.uk**

Hafford Letchfield, T, Leonard, K, Begum, N and Chick, N F (2008) *Leadership and management in social care.* London: Sage.

Hastings, M (2000) User involvement in education and training. In Pierce, R and Weinstein, J (eds) *Innovative education and training for care professionals.* London: Jessica Kingsley, 97–110.

Hawkins, P and Shohet, R (2000) *Supervision in the helping professions.* 2nd edition. Buckingham: Open University Press.

HCPC (2012) *Standards for proficiency for social work.* **www.hpc-uk.org**

Hofer, B K (2002) Personal epistemology as a psychological and educational construct: An introduction. In Hofer, B K and Pintrich, P R (eds) *Personal epistemology. The psychology of beliefs about knowledge and knowing.* Mahwah, NJ: Lawrence Erlbaum Associates Inc, 3–14.

Honey, P and Mumford, A (1982) *Manual of learning styles.* Maidenhead: Peter Honey.

Horwath, J (1999) It's not that I'm not good, it's just that I'm scared: Managing anxiety associated with practice learning. *Issues in Social Work Education,* 19 (1), 17–34.

Humphrey, C (2007) Observing students' practice (through the looking glass and beyond). *Social Work Education,* 26 (7), 723–36.

Humphries, B (2003) What else counts as evidence in evidence-based social work? *Social Work Education,* 22 (1), 81–91.

Ixer, G (1999) There is no such thing as reflection. *British Journal of Social Work,* 29, 513–27.

Jarvis, P (1992) Quality in practice: The role of education. *Nurse Education Today,* 21 (1), 3–10.

Juwah, C, Macfarlane-Dick, D, Matthew, B, Nicol, D, Ross, D and Smith, B (2004) *Enhancing student learning through effective formative feedback.* Higher Education Academy. **www.heacademy.ac.uk**

Kadushin, A and Harkness, D (2002) *Supervision in social work.* 4th edition. New York: Columbia University Press.

Kemp, E (2000) Partnership in the provision of education and training. In Pierce, R and Weinstein, J (eds) *Innovative education and training for care professionals.* London: Jessica Kingsley, 81–96.

Knott, C and Scragg, T (eds) (2010) *Reflective practice in social work.* 2nd edition. Exeter: Learning Matters.

Knowles, M (1980) *The modern practice of adult education. From pedagogy to andragogy.* 2nd edition. Englewood Cliffs: Prentice Hall/Cambridge.

Knowles, M (1990) *The adult learner – a neglected species.* 4th edition. London: Gulf Publishers.

Kolb, D A (1984) *Experiential learning. Experience as the source of learning and development.* New Jersey: Prentice Hall.

Kondrat, M E (1992) Reclaiming the practical: Formal and substantive rationality in social work practice. *Social Service Review,* 66 (2), 237–55.

Lafrance, J, Gray, E and Herbert, M (2004) Gate-keeping for professional social work practice. *Social Work Education,* 23 (3), 325–40.

Laming, Lord (2003) *The Victoria Climbié inquiry.* **www.nationalarchives.gov.uk/ERO/records /vc/1/1/finreport/finreport.htm**

Laming, Lord (2009)*The protection of children in England: A progress report.* London: The Stationery Office.

Lave, J and Wenger, E (1991) *Situated learning: Legitimate peripheral participation.* Cambridge: Cambridge University Press.

Lefevre, M (2005) Facilitating practice learning and assessment: The influence of social work education. *Social Work Education,* 24 (5), 565–83.

Levin, E (2004) *Resource guide 2: Involving service users and carers in social work education.* London: SCIE. **www.scie.org.uk/publications**

Lymbery, M (2009) Troubling times for British social work education? *Social Work Education,* 28 (8), 902–18.

Maclean, S and Lloyd, I (2008) *Developing quality practice learning in social work.* Rugeley: Kirwin Maclean Associates Ltd.

Marton, F, Hounsell, D and Entwistle, N J (1984) *The experience of learning.* Edinburgh: Scottish Academic Press.

Marton, F and Säljö, R (1976) On qualitative differences in learning: 1. Outcome and process. *British Journal of Educational Psychology,* 46, 4–11.

Maslow, A (1943) Theory of human motivation. *Psychological Review,* 50 (4), 370–96.

McGill, I and Beaty, L (1995) *Action learning. A guide for professional, management and educational development.* 2nd edition. London: Kogan Page.

Miettinen, R (2000) The concept of experiential learning and John Dewey's theory of reflective thought and action. *International Journal of Lifelong Education,* 19 (1), 54–72.

Moon, J (1999) *Reflection in learning and professional development.* London: Kogan Page.

Moon, J (2002) *Learning journals. A handbook for academics, students and professional development.* London: Kogan Page.

Moriarty, J, MacIntyre, G, Manthorpe, J, Crisp, B R, Orme, J, Lister P G, Cavanagh, K, Stevens, M, Hussein, S and Sharpe, E (2010) My expectations remain the same. The student has to be competent to practise. Practice assessor perspectives on the new social work degree qualification in England. *British Journal of Social Work,* 40, 583–601.

Mullins, L (2005) *Management and organisational behaviour.* 7th edition. Harlow: Prentice Hall.

Neary, M (2000) *Teaching, assessing and evaluation for clinical competence.* Cheltenham: Nelson Thornes.

Nixon, S and Murr, A (2006) Practice learning and the development of professional practice. *Social Work Education,* 25 (8), 798–811.

O'Hagan, K (1996) *Competence in social work practice.* London: Jessica Kingsley.

Parker, J (2004) *Effective practice learning in social work.* Exeter: Learning Matters.

Parker, J (2006) Developing perceptions of competence during practice learning. *British Journal of Social Work,* 36 (6), 1017–36.

Parker, J (2008) When things go wrong! Placement disruption and termination: Power and student perspectives. *British Journal of Social Work Advance Access,* November, 1–17.

Postle, K, Edwards, C, Moon, R, Rumsey, H and Thomas, T (2002) Continuing professional development after qualification – partnership, pitfalls and potential. *Social Work Education,* 21 (2), 157–69.

Prosser, M and Trigwell, K (1999) *Understanding learning and teaching. The experience in higher education.* Buckingham: SRHE and Open University Press.

QAAHE (2000) *Social policy and administration and social work: Subject benchmark statements.* Gloucester: Quality Assurance Agency for Higher Education.

Race, P (2010) *Making learning happen.* 2nd edition. London: Sage.

Ramsden, P (1992) *Learning to teach in higher education.* London: Routledge.

Rogers, A (2002) *Teaching adults.* 3rd edition. Buckingham: Open University Press.

Rogers, C R (1980) *Freedom to learn for the 80s.* New York: Free Press.

Rolfe, G, Freshwater, D and Jasper, M (2001) *Critical reflection for the nursing and helping professions. A user's guide.* London: Palgrave.

Ruch, G (2000) Self and social work: Towards an integrated model of learning. *Journal of Social Work Practice,* 14 (2), 99–112.

Säljö, R (1979) *Learning in the learner's perspective: 1: Some commonplace misconceptions.* Reports from the Institute of Education, University of Gothenburg, 76.

Schön, D (1983) *The reflective practitioner: How professionals think in action.* London: Temple Smith.

SCIE (2004) *Learning organisations. A self-assessment resource pack.* **www.scie.org.uk/public ations**

Senge, P (1990) *The fifth discipline: The art and practice of the learning organisation.* New York: Doubleday.

Shardlow, S I and Doel, M (1996) *Practice learning and teaching.* Basingstoke: Macmillan.

Sharp, M and Danbury, H (1999) *The management of failing DipSW students.* Aldershot: Ashgate.

Shaw, I (2004) Evaluating for a learning organisation? In Gould, N and Baldwin, M (eds) *Social work, critical reflection and the learning organisation.* Aldershot: Ashgate, 117–28.

Singh, G (2001) *Assessment in social work.* London: SCIE. **www.scie.org.uk**

Smedley, A, and Morey, P (2010) Improving learning in the clinical nursing environment: Perceptions of senior bachelor of nursing student. *Journal of Research in Nursing*, 15 (1), 75–88.

Smith, G (2003) Beyond critical thinking and decision making: teaching business students how to think. *Journal of Management Education*, 27(1), 24–51.

Smith, M K (1996, 2005) *The functions of supervision.* The Encyclopedia of Informal Education. **www.infed.org/biblio/functions_of_supervision.htm**

Smith, M K (2001) *David A Kolb on experiential learning.* The Encyclopedia of Informal Education. **www.infed.org/b-explrn.htm**

Social Work Task Force (2009) *Building a safe confident future.* London: Department of Health/ Department for Children, Schools and Families.

SWRB (2010) *Building a safe and confident future: one year on.* **www.education.gov.uk**

Taylor, C and White, S (2006) Knowledge and reasoning in social work: educating for humane judgement. *British Journal of Social Work*, 36, 937–54.

Thompson, N (2000) *Theory and practice in human services.* Buckingham: Open University Press.

Thompson, N (2005) *Understanding social work. Preparing for practice.* 2nd edition. London: Palgrave.

Thompson, N (2006) *Promoting workplace learning.* Bristol: Policy Press.

Thompson, S and Thompson, N (2008) *The critically reflective practitioner.* Basingstoke: Palgrave Macmillan.

Tisdell, E (1995) *Creating inclusive adult learning environments: Insights from multicultural education and feminist pedagogy.* Eric Information Series 361. Ohio: Ohio State University.

TOPSS (2002) *National occupational standards for social work.* TOPSS. **www.skillsforcare.org. uk**

Trevithick, P (2007) Revisiting the knowledge base of social work: A framework for practice. *British Journal of Social Work*, 37 (3), 1–26.

Tyreman, S (2000) Promoting critical thinking in health care: Phronesis and criticality. *Medicine, Health Care and Philosophy*, 3, 117–24.

University of York (2000) *Facts, feelings and feedback: A collaborative model for direct observation.* York: University of York.

Walker, J, Crawford, K and Parker, J (2008) *Practice education in social work: A handbook for practice teachers, assessors and educators.* Exeter: Learning Matters.

Webster-Wright, A (2009) Reframing professional development through understanding authentic professional learning. *Review of Educational Research*, 79 (2), 702–39.

Wenger, E (2000) Communities of practice and social learning systems. *Organization*, 2, 225–46.

Index

Learning Resources
Centre